To Alan and Sue,
With fond Regards,
John Chan[illegible]

[illegible]ov. 1981

Second Chance

John Charters

Second Chance

The true story of a man who 'died' and lived to describe the experience

GRANADA
London Toronto Sydney New York

Published by Granada Publishing 1980

Granada Publishing Limited
Frogmore, St Albans, Herts AL2 2NF
and
3 Upper James Street, London W1R 4BP
866 United Nations Plaza, New York, NY 10017, USA
117 York Street, Sydney, NSW 2000, Australia
100 Skyway Avenue, Rexdale, Ontario, M9W 3A6 Canada
PO Box 84165, Greenside, 2034, Johannesburg, South Africa
CML Centre, Queen & Wyndham, Auckland 1, New Zealand

ISBN 0 246 11141 0

Typeset by Cox & Wyman Ltd, Reading
Printed and bound in Great Britain by
Richard Clay (The Chaucer Press) Ltd, Bungay, Suffolk

Author's Note

This is a true story, although for obvious reasons some names have been changed. Not being a medical man, I have made no attempt to baffle the reader with science. I have put down my own impressions of exactly what happened, although a doctor might argue I could have been hallucinating because of drugs and medication. However, I have told it 'as it was'.

If this book helps any would-be suicide to reconsider, it will have been worthwhile.

To Monique

(alias Boggy Bogtail)

who made my second chance a happy reality

Part One

1

The stewardess had an angelic face and large virginal blue eyes which, as only English ladies can manage, gave a hint of unvirginal promises. From the waist down she was too heavy and had thick ankles. She checked our seat belts with the concentration of a nurse preparing her patient for a major operation.

The muted roar of the jet engines increased slowly as power was applied to the Rolls-Royce turbines. Near me sat an old Monsignor, enigmatically crossing himself as the big aircraft leapt forward, eager to shake off the confines of gravity. He smiled apologetically, as if ashamed of his lack of faith in God. Across the aisle, a middle-aged American matron, well fortified by dry martinis in the airport bar, tightly gripped a copy of *Vogue* and announced in a stage whisper, 'We'll never make it, it's Tuesday!'

Blessedly the rumbling stopped and the nose of the giant bird rose into the air, the hydraulics lifting up the landing gear until a soft thump announced the plane was streamlined into an object of beauty.

We shot through turbulent grey cloud and emerged into bright sunlight. The warning lights flicked off and a plummy British voice informed us we could smoke and that lunch would be served shortly. I loosened the seat belt and stretched out, wondering what lay in my future, if I had one.

Idly I pulled out my passport and studied it. It would need renewing in three months, must remember to remind my secretary, Aggie. It was well-travelled and showed the marks of many Immigration thumbs. In the closely-filled pages were the enthusiastic stamps marking entry to Paris, Rome, Madrid, Munich, Malta, Rabat, Cairo, Vienna and, on one page, an imposing visa giving me 'multiple' entries 'indefinitely' to the United States. On the second page I was listed as a 'Film Producer and Company Director', six feet one in height (my new passport would be in metres, no doubt?), with eyes of grey and fair hair.

It did not state that this hitherto healthy white male had recently undergone a tricky operation for deafness; that the operation had been reasonably successful apart from a loss of liquid in one ear, and that said white male suffered giddy spells and had a permanent imbalance. Even standing up had its own problems, and walking across a room without the aid of a stick or the help of a friendly chair or sofa required the utmost concentration.

'Your lunch, sir. Would you care for an aperitif?'

'A large vodka, please. On the rocks.'

She poured out the drink with a pretty smile. There were only four other passengers in the first-class section, so she was having an easy day.

'You're not eating, sir, can I bring you anything else?'

'No, it looks great. I just like to appreciate my vodka first. Then perhaps a little Beaujolais? I sound like an alcoholic!'

The meal was very good but my thoughts weren't. I had a difficult contract to negotiate with an Italian film producer and I was dreading the noise and bustle of Rome. Traffic now affected my balance and one bump from a pedestrian could knock me over; and with the effort of concentration needed to walk in a straight line it meant that by the end of a business day I was an exhausted wreck. It was no longer a joy to sample the delights of an Italian trattoria, as the chatter of fellow diners and the clatter of cutlery added to the confusion of my imbalance; I preferred to ring room service and eat in a tired silence.

A doctor and two specialists had been very sympathetic and totally unhelpful. Each one had eventually ended up with the same phrase, delivered with a professional smile. 'Unfortunate, yes, but you'll learn to live with it!' I didn't want to live with it, goddamit, to be a partial cripple and to be helped across the street; unable ever again to play golf or tennis, or dance or sail, or even take a country walk.

What were the chances of an operation to restore the missing magical liquid? None. Despite all modern science, there was no way of replacing what had been lost irretrievably.

'This is your Captain speaking. We have just passed over the island of Elba, and in a few minutes will commence our descent to Rome airport, where we expect to land in approximately sixteen minutes. The weather there is warm and sunny. We hope that you have enjoyed your flight...'

The aircraft banked slowly over Fregene, the sea below looking blue and inviting, the tiny white waves sharply etched like a Tomasoli painting. There was a brief protest from the massive tyres and then we were rumbling off the main runway up to the terminal. The lady across the aisle muttered a thankful 'Hallelujah!' and killed the last of a long line of martinis.

Reluctantly I stood up as the whine of the jets died away. For a brief moment the interior of the aircraft seemed to close in on me, then I was gripping the seat in front and fumbling for my walking-stick and briefcase. I made it safely to the exit and received a final sympathetic smile from the stewardess. She probably thought I had a wooden leg or had drunk too many vodkas. Paradoxically, alcohol minutely improved my balance, and the specialists had recommended it in reasonable quantities, although I was becoming tired of trying to explain this to people.

Going down the steps was not too difficult; I allowed the other passengers to precede me and hung on tightly to the rail. We had pulled up only a few metres from a ramp leading into the terminal, so I did not have the problem of climbing into a bus and being jogged by hot, impatient passengers. I started the perilous journey across to the ramp, trying to keep my balance with the aid of the walking-stick, feeling the hot sun beating down and causing shimmering waves of heat to reflect from the blinding tarmac to confuse me further.

I reached the ramp and thankfully clutched the rail up the side. By now, my fellow-travellers had surged inside and I was virtually alone. At the top of the incline I turned and surveyed the airport, wondering how much longer I could go on bluffing the world; a man with one leg receives immediate sympathy and assistance, but a perfectly healthy-looking specimen like myself could hardly go around with a notice saying DON'T TOUCH ME OR I'LL FALL OVER. The fierce glare of the afternoon sun made the vertigo worse, and carefully I turned and walked inside the terminal.

The journey across the wide floor to the Immigration Control was another nightmare. Everyone was rushing somewhere, and the mere presence of so many moving people taxed my brain signals to the utmost. When I reached the queue of passengers I felt weak and unsteady and, despite the air-conditioning, the perspiration was soaking my back.

An elderly American motioned me in front of him. 'You look mighty pale, friend, you feeling okay? You go first, I've all the time in the world.'

Through Immigration, I sat on a luggage trolley on the periphery of the milling crowd and waited for my cases. As soon as I was sitting life seemed better. I hoped the car I had ordered would be waiting outside; after that I only had to negotiate the swing doors of the Grand Hotel and cross the lobby, register, find the elevator, and walk down the long corridor to my room. Then the blessed moment when I could lie flat on the bed and feel normal again.

In retrospect, it sounded simple. But it was a knife in the back to a film producer's career, where speed and versatility of movement were the very life-blood of a successful contract.

It had started two years previously when I realized I was becoming deaf. Small symptoms, like turning up the sound on television until my wife winced; watching the 'rough cut' of a film and complaining to the technical engineer I couldn't hear the dialogue; setting up the finance for a film with my bankers (who always discuss money in hushed voices); assuming my watch had stopped because I could not hear it tick.

Eventually I visited an ear specialist who made some audio tests and confirmed that both ears were slightly 'down'. He advised a simplified hearing aid if it became worse.

It did. Another few months and I was straining to hear a normal conversation. It affected my work. Being in the film business, I liked to see almost every new film. Now it was mental agony to visit a cinema and miss most of the dialogue. My colleagues complained I was speaking loudly, a sure symptom of going deaf.

I consulted a famous ear specialist and he recommended a new operation called a stapedectomy, where half or all of the 'foot-plate' is removed and then replaced with stainless steel or plastic. I understood none of this, but decided to have the operation.

It was a great success. Nobody who has not suffered from deafness can know the sweetness of having the ear dressings removed and suddenly hearing the noise of traffic outside, the ticking of a bedside clock, the rustle of a pillow against the ear. Even one ear. In a few weeks I felt younger and more alive; I no longer had to strain and concentrate to hear what was being said, nor suffer the frustration and embarrassment of trying to cover up my affliction.

The other ear became increasingly deaf, and finally I returned to the specialist and asked him to operate on it.

I arranged to take a week off from my office, and entered the hospital with a light heart. Although the operation was a lengthy one, there was no pain when I woke up and, apart from a few days dizziness, no unpleasant after-effects. That evening I reckoned I was a very lucky man. I was forty-eight, with an attractive young wife, a successful business, and in a few hours I would have perfect hearing again. Before going to sleep on the eve of the operation I had performed my nightly ritual of touching my toes twenty-four times.

I never dreamed it would be for the last time.

It was two weeks before I suspected something was wrong. I could hear perfectly in both ears, but I had been kept in the hospital because the post-operative giddiness had not yet disappeared, and I still had to call a nurse to lean on when I went to the toilet. It was most irritating. I felt fine as long as I was sitting, or in bed, but the moment I stood up the walls spun round. Only with an effort could I walk across the room, like a hopeless drunk.

I was given a variety of pills, none of which helped. My office was now phoning frantically every day, as decisions had to be made and delays are a film producer's nightmare. One day the surgeon came to see me, jolly as ever.

'Malingering still, eh? Well, we're sending you home. A little rest and then you'll be back at the grindstone!'

'Marvellous,' I said, 'but I've had all the rest I need, and it requires an awful lot of balance to stay on that old grindstone.'

'Nothing to worry about, old chap, possibly there was a slight leak of perilymph which has resulted in this delay in recovering your balance.'

I had no idea who Perry Lymph was, but being a good patient I believed him. I rejected the hospital's offer of an ambulance and my wife drove me home.

For a terrifying three weeks I was unable to leave the house. The actual giddiness improved slowly, and after a few days I was able to stand and walk without falling over. I had been given a walking-stick and was able to move around slowly, provided I did not turn my head suddenly or look upwards. Gradually I learnt to use my stick like an extra limb. As I was to hear many times in the future, I was learning to live with it.

I felt like a decrepit old man.

2

I relaxed on the large bed in the Grand Hotel and mentally reviewed my life over the past eighteen months since I'd had that second operation. It had been traumatic in more ways than one.

My whole mode of life had changed. I had turned from an easy-going executive into a bitter, humourless man who had rejected almost all his friends. I had become a cripple, both physically and mentally.

Unexpectedly, my lovely wife Gloria left me. I suppose I cannot blame her. We had been married only three years and she was twenty years younger than I was; and she had married a healthy specimen who liked to entertain. We had had a rip-roaring time, attending glamorous first-nights, giving dinner parties, dancing in smart night clubs, skiing in Klosters in the winter, flying to warm locations when I was making a film, meeting celebrities and being invited to all the 'in' parties. Suddenly I was a morose creature, bad company and bad-tempered.

I commuted between my office and the house. For lunch I had sandwiches at my desk and for dinner I had a freezer full of revolting TV dinners which I stuck in the oven and often forgot. I had always drunk in moderation but now I could dispose of a bottle of whisky a day with no trouble. It helped my balance a little and eased the need of concentration just to walk across a room. My golf clubs remained in the closet and my tennis racket gathered dust.

Sadly, my jolly surgeon had died suddenly of a heart attack. I visited his successor, also a well-known ear specialist, who had been of little encouragement. Doctors always stick together, but there was little doubt that he felt my own specialist should never have carried out the second operation. He, too, tried several more anti-vertigo pills on me, with no success. Definitely, the liquid in the middle ear had been lost or leaked during the second operation, and my balance would never return to normal.

People were kind and sympathetic, which made it worse. The last thing I needed was pity; it seemed to rub in the fact that I was no longer 'normal', like a man who has gone blind or lost both legs in an accident. I behaved like a stupid boor, my usually eclectic outlook now narrowed and resentful. Gradually friends and colleagues ceased to visit what had previously been 'open house'.

My situation had deteriorated until one night, only four months previously, I had felt so depressed I had opened a second bottle of Scotch. By eleven o'clock I was high and hungry. Discarding my usual caution in a fit of drunken zeal, I walked into the kitchen without my stick, banged my shoulder against the doorpost, lost my balance and fell with a crash which must have rocked the building. My head hit the leg of the kitchen table and a black wave of unconsciousness lifted up and I crept gratefully under it.

Luckily for me my assistant, Josh Camber, working late on a script, decided to telephone me for advice on a tricky point. Getting no reply and knowing that I never retired early, he walked round from his own apartment nearby. I had taken to leaving the front door unlocked until I went to bed, it saved me making laborious journeys from the study where I worked. He found me in a pool of blood and promptly called an ambulance.

As it happened, it was much ado about very little. I had cut my head slightly and had to have three stitches put in.

But Josh was an earnest young man and was obviously very worried about my condition. I did not go to the office the next day, and that afternoon was surprised to see an extraordinary looking priest walk into the sitting-room where I was re-reading a script.

He waved a hand apologetically. 'Sorry to interrupt, man, but Josh told me to come straight in. Understand you don't get around much any more, just like the old cornball song says. My name's Pete. The Reverend Peter Smythe-Watson, can you imagine? But everyone calls me Pete.'

He was quite young, not over thirty, with a black goatee beard and a drooping Mexican-style moustache. Long hair tumbled down his neck, partly hiding the clerical collar. He could have been a hippy directly out of Piccadilly Circus, except that his hair was clean and neatly combed.

I wasn't particularly happy to see him. My days of religion were far behind me. I was in my late teens during the war, and saw enough action to make me wonder what God was thinking about or trying to prove. My best friend was blown to smithereens in front of me and I helped to scrape up bits of bone and skin; another time when on leave I was in bed with a most attractive girl with whom I was half in love. The sirens sounded, and the anti-aircraft guns started up. We were hastily dressing when a stray piece of shrapnel screamed through the window, passed through my girl friend and buried itself in the wall. I watched while her intestines snaked out of a huge cut across her stomach. Never will I forget the silent pleading look on her face as she tried uselessly to hold herself together.

I must have been staring at the priest in an unfriendly manner. His mouth split into a wide grin, showing very white teeth.

'C'mon, man, I'm not gonna bite you. Josh felt you needed cheering up, so here I am. I gotta great collection of jokes and funny stories. Or we can discuss the metaphysics of the neutron bomb, or maybe you prefer Barth, Updike or Barbara Raskin? I can quote long passages of the Bible, too. I'm a fucking genius.'

It caught me unawares and I burst out laughing. There was something refreshing about this weird character and I supposed his was the right way to appeal to the modern generation. Jesus and Peace and Flower Power and pot were all very well, but the youngsters would never make the effort of entering a church unless it was to listen to one of their own. I rather liked Peter Smythe-Watson.

'So, Father,' I said with a touch of irony, as he was probably twenty years younger than me, 'you've come to cheer me up. I don't need cheering up, I just want a nice small miracle. How about that?'

'They come expensive, man! And I don't mean loot.'

'You mean faith?'

He shrugged, his large black eyes unblinking.

'Hot damn! That's a big word, faith. You ever tried it? I mean, *really* tried it, not just talked about it.'

'If you mean in a religious way, no. I'm afraid I gave up believing in God some time ago. I prefer to put my faith in doctors and surgeons. Although they haven't done such a great job either. That's not fair, I suppose, at least I'm not deaf any more.'

Pete took an upright Hepplewhite and sat astride it.

'Josh tells me you had two operations. Mobilizations or stapedectomies?'

I looked at him in surprise. I knew enough about my own affliction to know that the mobilization operation, a great advance a few years ago, was now considered obsolete. Pete seemed to be a man of many parts. Again he grinned as he saw my look.

'I studied medicine for four years; wanted to be a great surgeon and save the world. Then I decided I could save the world in a better way. I'm not really a religious man, I just love people and I know in my own silly way I can often straighten them out and help them.'

'But you must believe in God, then?'

'Only in an abstract way. I don't believe he's sitting up there on a cloud listening to the woes of six hundred million humans, let alone all the other planets. To me, God is way inside me, he's a little bit of myself, my alter ego, who I can talk to and argue with and maybe sometimes take his advice if I think he's right. But I don't give him a capital "H" when I write about him. I respect him but I don't worship him, because he's really a little part of me; and I'm no great shakes.'

I had never listened to such a theory, especially from a clergyman. I liked Pete even more.

'So, no miracles! You have any suggestions?'

'Yeah, man. Get off your arse and stop feeling fucking sorry for yourself!'

Remembering that first meeting with Pete, I was laughing silently when the vodka and tonic I had ordered from 'Room Service' arrived. I tipped the waiter and took a long, slow drink. Pete had been right, although at the time I had been furious. But the next day I returned to the office in a different frame of mind. Other people had suffered sudden tragedies or illnesses and been able to conquer them, why not me? To everyone's delight, I announced we were going back into production, a script entitled *Misty Horizon*, which I had bought two years previously. I hadn't liked either the title or the screenplay, but the underlying plot was excellent, and once you have a good plot you should be able to write a fine screenplay.

My last two films had made a fair amount of money, and my share of the profits was now dribbling in. Although my overheads were heavy (I liked to keep a good staff on permanent salary, whether we were actually filming or not), I decided to hire a chauffeur to drive me to and from the office. Although I was perfectly capable of driving, as I was sitting down, my office in Brook Street had no parking facilities, and normally I left the car in a nearby public garage. With a chauffeur, I could avoid the difficult walk from the garage.

For a few weeks I immersed myself in work, driving to distraction the two writers working on the final script. The action of *Misty Horizon* took place mainly in Italy and

Spain, with the beginning and ending in London. It was ideal for a tri-part co-production, with each country putting up a proportion of the production costs; and with luck I might be able to arrange that each country obtained a 'quota' permit, enabling it to apply for Government aid, usually about eighteen per cent of the gross box-office takings.

During that time I did not fool myself that I was happy. Each day was a struggle, and every time I stood up I felt a pang of pure despair as I waited the two or three seconds for the room to steady. I had to learn never to turn my head suddenly, and to keep my eyes fixed on the ground about six feet in front of me. I found just a light touch on the back of a chair, or my fingertips brushing against a wall, gave enormous help to my equilibrium. My worst enemies were traffic, jostling pedestrians, and loud music.

And now here I was, in Rome, hoping to complete the negotiations which I had been carrying out by letters and telephone calls over the past month. Theoretically, the meeting tomorrow would be the signing of final contracts between my company and the Italian distributing company who would also put up the money for the portion of the film shot in Rome. But I knew from past experience that there would be last-minute objections and haggling; details impossible to resolve by telephone.

Josh had wanted to come with me, but a stubborn streak of pride made me turn down his sensible offer. I had always finalized these deals alone, and much as I liked Josh, I did not want to feel I was dependent on him. Now I regretted my decision. He would have been invaluable at this moment.

It was time for my first meeting. Usually on these occasions I took a suite in the hotel and persuaded people to come to me, on the pretence I was a visitor with no time to waste being stuck in Rome's eternal traffic jams. But today the final meeting was to be held at the Tiberio offices, in view of the large number of people attending.

Del Pardini, my Italian co-producer, had arranged to pick me up in his car. He was waiting in the foyer, and, as usual, he was in bubbling good spirits. In the car on the way to the meeting he explained the possible complications which lay ahead.

'Is the ending they not like. Too sad, they want the lovers should live, not die. I tell them is the whole point of the story, otherwise is old-fashioned corn.'

'Well, for sure I'm not altering the ending. Can you imagine *Love Story* with the girl suddenly recovering? And why are they bringing this up now? They approved the final script weeks ago.'

'Is true, but always there is someone who wants to impress the boss. *Probabile* the sister of the wife of the elevator man read the script and cried, and now Demanio scared!' Demanio was the autocratic head of Tiberio Studios and distribution. But Del Pardini had summed up the situation well. Demanio had been known to give a script to his tea-trolley lady, in order to get a 'common touch' reaction. But *Misty Horizon* was a tear-jerker in the old style, which would require brilliant direction and a high calibre of acting; to have a happy ending would reduce it to a cheap second-rate movie.

I sank into one of Demanio's huge leather armchairs in his palatial office and hoped the meeting would not drag on the entire evening. The two representatives from La Banca di Roma, which was financing part of the film, I knew fairly well. They were tough negotiators, but provided Demanio gave his guarantee, there would be no problems from them. Tiberio's team of lawyers was also present, two older men and one youngster, all experts on production budgets and distribution contracts; Roberto Blasio, Demanio's production supervisor, a hatchet man with no personal emotions whose sole job was to ensure that a film kept to schedule and within the budget; my own lawyer, a shrewd and experienced film *avvocato* who was bi-lingual, a most important factor when hundred-page contracts had to be written in both English and Italian; and Demanio, Del Pardini, and myself.

We spoke in Italian. Most of the conversation I could

follow with ease, relying on my lawyer to translate any obscure legal points. In one hour we disposed of all the minor items which had not already been agreed upon by letter or telephone. Eventually the bankers and Demanio's lawyers were dismissed, their services no longer being required. I breathed a sigh of relief; at least there were no unforeseen snags in the actual contract. Now we turned to the artistic side of the film.

'Your casting suggestions were excellent, dear sir,' Demanio proclaimed in his regal manner, 'are they contracted?'

'Of course not.' I said it more sharply than I meant. I was already tired from the trip and was dreading the evening ahead. In the car Del Pardini had told me he was giving a cocktail party in my honour. This meant it would start at ten o'clock; it was the last 'honour' I needed. 'You have the right to approve the first three stars above the title. If you approve of my suggestions, I will cable their agents at once. All I know is that they were available about a week ago when I put in the inquiries.'

'Good! Now, about the ending.' Demanio offered round a box of Monte Cristos, a casual peace-offering which fooled no one. 'I feel that these days we have too many downbeat films with unhappy endings. The public comes to a cinema to be entertained, to leave with a happy feeling. Admittedly, he likes to see as many disasters as possible, but at the end the hero must claim his heroine. Then Mister Public will go home happy, and more important, come back the next week.' He said all this in Italian, of course, using his full Florentine upbringing and speaking the flowery words with beautiful articulation. But the smell of distribution money was even more powerful than the cigar smoke. I struggled to my feet, tightly grasping my stick until the ceiling came to a halt.

'Signor Demanio,' I said very quietly, 'you must forgive me if I appear impolite, but I have been ill and find myself very fatigued. I have spent nearly four months with two brilliant writers on this project, and under no circumstances will there be a happy ending to this film. It would destroy the entire structure of the story; it would be unrealistic, miracles do not happen in real life, not even to please distributors. The irony of the whole relationship, of the whole story, is that after he is killed in the car crash it is *she* who becomes the alcoholic. The motive is sound and the reasoning is credible. Of *course* it's a sad film, but I believe it will be a great film if we get this cast. There won't be a dry eye in the cinema and, believe me, that can be good box office too. Is there anything else we have to discuss?'

Demanio stood up slowly, tapping his lips with a pencil. He crossed to the big windows and peered out, seeing nothing. He was a big man, a born dictator, accustomed to having his own way, which I had to admit was usually right. Normally, I would have been much more tactful in my negotiations with him, but somehow I knew that my career as a film producer was almost finished; if I managed to produce *Misty Horizon* it would be the kind of miracle of which Pete would approve.

Abruptly Demanio turned and held out his hand, a wide smile on his face. 'You are right! Always I liked the sad ending, but my wife cried in bed for two hours after reading it. I hope the audience cries too. We will give out free paper tissues to every lady entering the cinema.'

'Santo cielo! Ma guarda chi si vede! Non ti si vede da un bel po'.'

'Nadia Nerone! Bellissima come sempre! Vivi ancora a Roma?'

'Si, mi va molto bene, ho molto lavoro. Abita sempre a Londra?'

'Si, ma questa città mi manca molto. Che bel tempi che erano!'

It was past eleven, and Del Pardini's lovely sitting-room had french windows opening on to a patio and pool. Many of the guests were outside, where a long bar had been set up to cope with the overflow. I had been sitting on the edge of an armchair when I recognized the girl in the long black satin dress, tightly waisted and leaving her shoulders bare. Ten years ago it would have been fashionable, but nevertheless it looked sensational on her tall, slim figure. Nadia was probably now thirty-five, but appeared much younger. She was married to an Italian actor with whom I had many times skied.

'How's Carlo? Is he here?'

She made a little moue with her attractive mouth. 'I have no idea. We split up a year ago, he's living with an eighteen-year-old blonde with long pigtails. We're all good friends. How's Gloria?'

I told her that we, too, had parted. I explained why, although it didn't make much sense when one talks about an 'imbalance' being a reason for divorce. She shook her head sadly.

'But you and Gloria were made for each other! You had so much fun together, always joking! How could she possibly have left you?'

'What about you and Carlo? I always pointed you out as the perfect example of an actor and actress being able to live happily together. What went wrong?'

She shrugged her shoulders, the tight black satin gleaming sexily in the lights. 'The usual thing. I started to get better parts than he was being offered. Then he had a long spell without any work at all, and I was away on location. He met this girl in his agent's office, and she started to console him, in the classic manner. Besides, he's always liked Lolita types, and I must confess she's an absolute honey.'

For a moment we stared at each other. There had always been a mutual attraction between us, but because of our respective partners we had never acknowledged it. Now it seemed that fate was up to its tricks. I could feel the old beast stirring, my sex life had been neglected for months, and suddenly I urgently wanted this desirable creature.

Her smile was both coy and seductive. 'I came with a young director who's considering me for a leading role in his next film. I told him I never mix business with pleasure and there's no chance of his getting a quick lay. But I like to leave a party with the same man who brings me. Shall we have a drink in the bar at your hotel in say an hour? You're at the Grand as usual?'

It was almost twelve when I made my excuses to leave and accepted Del Pardini's offer to let his chauffeur drive me to the hotel. My depression had returned and on the way back I wondered whether I had any right to take on the responsibility of producing *Misty Horizon.* I was juggling and being entrusted with a project which would cost nearly three million dollars. Not a large budget for a film by modern standards, but I knew that the next nine months would be purgatory for me. Producing a film is absolute hell when one is fit and alert; in my afflicted condition, with exhaustion my constant companion, I began to have serious doubts about my physical ability to follow through on the cutting, editing, scoring, dubbing and hundred other details before the film would be ready for public viewing.

I tried to cheer myself up by remembering people who were much worse off than myself. My local butcher, a happy, jolly fellow, had been knocked over by a hit-and-run driver. He had suffered a fractured spine; within three months he was back in his shop, in a wheelchair, cheerful as ever.

The bar of the hotel was almost empty and Pietro was already putting up the side shutters of the long counter. I ordered a small vodka and wondered if Nadia would turn up. She was already ten minutes late. My sexual uprising of an hour before had dissipated, leaving only a longing to lie down and sleep forever. Perchance to dream; aye, there's the rub! For in my dreams I was always alert and normal and planning great schemes, my brain racing ahead to demonstrate what vast projects could—

'Hi! Did you think I wasn't coming?'

She stood there wrapped in mink, despite the summer evening. I stood up quickly and nearly fell over. She caught my arm.

'Steady! Bacchus is not your friend.'

Annoyance washed over me, why did everyone always assume I was drunk? We sat down and Pietro came across for last orders.

'It's not alcohol,' I told her quietly, 'I have a balance problem ...' I explained briefly my ear operation. I don't think she was listening, her eyes were sparkling and she laid a gloved hand on my knee.

'All talk and no action,' she whispered, 'can we take our drinks upstairs with us?'

Weird, the sexual impulse lurking in our minds, an uninhibited beast waiting to spring upon the soft bands of tolerance. My spirits soared and in one second she had restored my confidence and self-esteem. All was fine with the world and I consigned my imbalance to the rear of my brain.

In my room, she slipped out of the mink and let me fondle her slim body in the shining satin, emitting low moans as my hands played upon her like a finely-tuned violin. She broke away and disappeared into the bathroom. Carefully I undressed and put on a silk gown, then poured out some cognac I always carried in a flask.

She returned wearing only the top of my pyjamas, the sleeves rolled up and looking tomboyish and utterly desirable. She accepted the proffered glass and slid into the big double bed. Somehow it all seemed perfectly natural, as if we had carried through the same routine many times in the past. To Nadia, perhaps it was only a night's flirtation, a quick lay which would satisfy her sexual appetite until she found the right man again and entered into a more lasting relationship. For me, it had a deeper connotation. Apart from the fact she was a very attractive girl, I felt this very act would prove to me I could still lead a full and satisfying life. Golf and tennis might be out, but it was not the end of the world; I was, after all, approaching fifty, and no longer was there a need to prove anything – not even to myself.

Her long dark hair spilled over the pillow. She smiled at me and reached out a bare arm to turn off the lights. In the darkness I slipped out of my dressing-gown and approached the bed, forgetting that a third of one's balance is controlled through the eyes. Suddenly I was falling in the darkness; my knee caught the edge of the double bed and I fell heavily across her. She gave a grunt of pain.

I pushed myself on to my back and spun into pitch black vertigo, floating in an abyss of bewildering space, trying desperately to focus and stay conscious. I groped for the light switch which would bring blessed sanity back to my brain. I tried to speak, to explain, to cry out for help, but I was in a black world of my own and I dimly heard muffled grunts coming from my throat.

I lay there for a few minutes, utterly exhausted and unable even to switch on the light. I felt myself tumbling over and over in space and didn't dare open my eyes. Vaguely I felt Nadia rise from the bed, then the distant sound of running water in the bathroom. I became aware of light in the room, but my eyes were locked shut. I heard the door open and close, then a shattering silence.

Once again I was alone.

I lay there for a long time. It was during those unhappy hours that the first thoughts of suicide occurred to me.

I feel it's important that you don't think of me as one of those manic-depressives who drinks a bottle of Scotch and at five in the morning decides life isn't worth living, and either shoots out his brains or cuts his wrists. I have always been a most practical, down-to-earth person, and I've always pitied people who committed suicide as being weak idiots; yes, and despised them as well, because there is so much in life to appreciate.

The idea of suicide came to me in vague, impersonal moments over a period of months. At first I did not take myself seriously, it was merely an academic thought; I knew I could never commit the act. But gradually it became more logical.

Usually the most despicable thing about a suicide is the selfishness of it. It brings pain and suffering and guilt to parents and close friends, to wife and children. It employs the services of doctors, ambulance men, morticians and a coroner, who could all be more gainfully using their valuable time. I had an advantage here. My parents were dead and I had no close relatives alive. Gloria had departed and was now happily ensconced with a young and successful banker in the City who wore trendy clothes and had a large expense account. So, apart from my immediate colleagues in the office, most of whom were alienated by my recent behaviour and surliness, there was no one who would be hurt if I killed myself.

I was being perfectly logical in my approach. I had lived a good life, and I did not want to become a burden on society and a useless old man; and, probably, an alcoholic.

I slept little that night and was up early, depression and tiredness uniting to form a pounding headache. Somehow I wanted to apologize to Nadia, to explain I was not drunk, but I knew how lame my excuses would sound. To her, I had fallen across the bed and passed out, humiliating both of us. It had been a sorry end to what could have been a highly-charged night of eroticism. I did not even know her address, to send flowers. Wearily, I ordered coffee and rolls and tried to concentrate on the day ahead.

I flew to Madrid on the two o'clock Iberia flight. A meeting had been arranged for nine o'clock the next morning for the signing of the Spanish side of the film.

The co-producer, José Don Fellino, sent his car to Madrid airport to bring me to the Ritz Hotel, with a note of apology that he was tied up in a meeting and would expect me for dinner at nine o'clock.

Half-way across the huge foyer of the Ritz a waiter came steaming towards me carrying a tray of drinks in one expert hand. Feeling exposed and unsteady I stopped abruptly to let him pass, just as he decided to weave behind me. We met with a horrifying crash, and next minute I was lying on the expensive Ritz carpet with a mixture of Scotch and gin gently soaking through my trousers.

Don Fellino was an elderly, highly successful producer and distributor, one of the bastions of the Spanish film industry. A member of the aristocracy, he was reputed to be worth a small fortune.

His chauffeur who had brought me from the airport had arranged to pick me up at 8.45. Several guests had already arrived, and I was shown into the magnificent library where drinks were being served.

Don Fellino came over to me, frowning with a judicious air which made him even more like James Mason than usual.

'I hear you have not been well, my friend. You have lost weight and now carry a cane. It is nothing serious?'

I gave him a brief rundown, including the fact that Gloria and I had split. He regarded me with sad eyes, a typical Spanish nobleman who took a friend's problems upon himself. He had met Gloria several times, and had always been amused at her vivacity and sense of humour.

'But this – imbalance, you call it? – Surely it must become better? You cannot go through life like that, you are too young and strong. How will you be able to carry on your work?'

He had put his finger on the nerve centre. It was essential he did not lose confidence in my ability to produce *Misty Horizon*. He was, after all, putting up one-third of the budget. I liked him immensely, but he was still a very tough business man. Better to denigrate my illness.

'You're right, it will pass soon. Meanwhile I carry a stick as a psychological prop. Shortly I hope to throw it away.'

Abruptly he left me and strode over to an ornate desk in the corner. He wrote rapidly on a piece of paper, then returned and handed it to me.

'Forgive me if I seem to interfere. Some years ago I, too, started to go deaf. It was most embarrassing. I came to London and consulted this gentleman. He is a specialist, and he cured me. Would you do me the favour of at least talking to him?'

Inwardly I sighed, although I appreciated his concern. Some of the best Ears, Nose and Throat specialists had charged me exorbitant fees to assure me there was nothing to be done. But I took the piece of paper and thanked him sincerely for the introduction.

'He is a strange man, he worked in the Far East for many years. He is a great believer in acupuncture and the mind healing the body. Tell him you have come from me, and at least listen to what he says.'

I promised to do so, which was the biggest mistake I ever made. Later at the hotel I took out the note and read it.

The name of the specialist was Professor John Remon-Jarrett, with an address in Hampstead.

As I had hoped, there were no hold-ups the next morning at Don Fellino's office. The contracts were signed and exchanged within an hour. I caught the afternoon flight and arrived at Heathrow in a thunderstorm, the rain roiling down from a churning overcast sky.

I arrived at the apartment, exhausted even by the short journey, and poured out a large vodka over ice, savouring the sting and oily taste of the Polish drink. Then I glanced through the accumulated mail. There was a Western Union cable.

I read it slowly, cursing long and blasphemously. The male star I wanted for the film was no longer available.

Now my troubles were starting. I would have to send through another script to the States for another 'name' actor, probably waiting four weeks for a reply. Meanwhile I would have to obtain approval from the Italian and Spanish distributors, and further confirmation from the female star, who usually had the right to approve her male co-star.

Worst of all, it would entail another round-trip to alter and re-sign all the contracts.

Enormously depressed again, I went to bed.

Professor John Remon-Jarrett had given me a thorough examination and had earnestly studied my official case-history file. He was a big man, in his sixties, with flashing false teeth and a pompous manner. He had thick white hair and an incongruous small tuft of a beard. He sat behind a large desk and pressed his fingers together as if lecturing a class of imbecile students.

'A most interesting case. Yes indeed. The double stapedectomy is most unusual, most unusual. Yet it has worked very well, your hearing is only slightly impaired, in the higher ranges. You had no pain after the second operation?'

'No. Only the giddiness which, unlike the first time, did not disappear after a week or so.'

'Yes. A pity. You *do* have a balance problem.'

After a year of staggering around, he was telling me nothing new.

'My friend Don Fellino hoped you might have some constructive suggestions.'

He waved a hand in the air. 'The loss of the perilymph is most regrettable. Most regrettable. Unfortunately, there is no way to replace it. However, the main damage may have been caused in the inner ear during the operation. No way to tell.'

'I've tried several anti-vertigo pills. They didn't help at all.'

'No, they wouldn't. They work on a different section of the aural composition. There is no cure for your malady.'

At least he was honest, even if the visit had been a waste of time.

'Tell me, Professor, will I gradually get used to it, so that I can get around more easily? I've been told several times that I'll "learn to live with it".'

He smiled mechanically, the executioner responding to the doomed man's last joke.

'You can learn to live with almost anything. I'm afraid you must face the fact it will probably become worse as you grow older.'

An icy knot formed in my stomach. None of the other specialists had even hinted at this.

'Get worse? Just what does that mean?'

Now his faded blue eyes were fixed on a spot above my head. 'I'm afraid that within five years you may find it necessary to get about in a wheelchair, if you go outside. Otherwise it will be dangerous to you. Inside your house you will still be able to live a fairly normal life. You will be able to attend to your toilet needs by yourself, even dress yourself if you keep sitting down. It will necessitate your re-forming your way of life to adapt to your new environment.'

He continued to talk, but the words floated aimlessly over my head. A wheelchair! How the hell could I continue in my business in a wheelchair! I was aware that I had stood up and was shaking hands with him as he led me to the door. He paused before opening it.

'You are almost fifty and have led an active life. If a man has a heart attack he must learn to adjust his way of living accordingly. If a man loses his sight, the future will seem hopeless until he becomes used to the change, adapts himself accordingly. He will compensate by becoming immersed in music, and appreciate the smell of autumn and the scent of good coffee; the man with a heart attack will play chess instead of tennis, eat toast instead of cream buns. Be thankful you will not be a helpless cripple. Your heart is strong, you may have many years ahead of you. Now you must trust in God.'

I walked slowly down the street, vaguely looking for a taxi, my mind still not grasping the appalling ramifications of his diagnosis. Already in my imagination I could feel the creeping malignance becoming worse, the effort to stand and walk becoming more difficult, the fear of falling over becoming reality. I felt like the hero in a B picture who has been told he has six months to live.

The idea of suicide was no longer academic.

3

From the moment we are born, each day is one day nearer death. Not very original; I had read it in a book years before and thought what a witless and asinine statement it was; now I was not so sure.

I had never been afraid of dying but, being a comparative coward, I had always been afraid of dying in agony. As a child I had suffered from severe earache, and even now I could recall the blinding pain which would sometimes stab through my head, followed by hours of intense aching which no oils or heat could assuage. At the age of ten I was carted off to a nursing home and operated on for a double mastoid, in those days a serious operation which could be fatal. Every day I became hysterical when the doctor or nurse came to change the dressings; the pain was so intense I had to be held down forcibly, and for months afterwards even the mention of our doctor's name would send me into fits of sobbing.

I found a taxi and for no particular reason told him to drop me off in Berkeley Square. It was a fine day and the sun shone benignly on scantily-clad office girls taking their lunch break. I felt curiously numb and wrapped in my own misery, for I knew now that I was passing my own death sentence.

I had no intention of becoming an embittered old man in a wheelchair, cut off from the world, unable to go out without assistance, severed from my work and living in isolation. Nor would I inflict my misery on anyone else. If I'd had a loving wife it might have been different, but Gloria was young and had departed, and I would not try to bring her back through pity.

I paid off the taxi and walked slowly to the bottom of the Square gardens. The big statue was still there, the one I had played round when my nanny used to bring me here for an afternoon outing. My parents had taken a house in Curzon Street when I was five years old, and it was strange to remember I had played in this very spot more than forty years earlier, unaware of what life was about or how I would stumble through it. I sat on a bench, feeling relaxed and much happier now that I had made the big decision.

I was sorry about *Misty Horizon,* but I was certain it would still get produced. Warner Brothers had been interested in the original story, and I would attempt to sell the property to them, making my colleagues part of the deal, so that no one would suffer financially from my exit. Much planning would be necessary, and I would have to be very careful not to arouse suspicion. In fact, it would be like producing a new play, which I had not done for over ten years. I would give myself one month until opening – and closing – night. Four weeks in which to put my affairs in order, make a will, tidy up my life so that I could step into the unknown with a clear conscience.

Saturday evening, one month from now. It must be the week-end: less chance of any interference from outside sources.

Four weeks, actually twenty-nine days, as today was Friday. I sat in the sunlight and tried to remember a film I had seen years before, where the star knew (for some forgotten reason) that he would be assassinated in six weeks. He had planned a bewildering schedule for himself, to do everything he had always wanted to do, in the limited time which remained.

Travel was out. I had been almost everywhere in the world during my career as film producer; and besides, it was no pleasure to travel now. To eat well? Certainly, but I was already spoiled with years of entertaining backers and film stars in the best restaurants. Drinking expensive wines? Yes, but ditto. Sex? My recent experience in Rome made me cautious, nor did I want to start up a relationship where the girl would be shocked and hurt by my suicide.

Suicide! Now the word had a personal ring to it, and for a moment I thought how bloody silly I was to be sitting there planning to kill myself. But upon reflection I could see no good reason not to do so, and every motive for it.

So what did I want to accomplish in those four weeks? The Vienna Symphony Orchestra was coming to the Albert Hall to give a Mozart concert, my favourite composer. In the programme they were to play the Concerto No. 21 in C, again one of my favourites. I would try to obtain a box, to avoid the embarrassment of tripping and falling over people's feet in the stalls. I had not had time to attend a race meeting for years, I would take a day off to drive to one of the courses and have a mild flutter. And a morning at the Tate Gallery – again pressure of work had meant giving up my bi-annual visits there; and if I took it slowly it would not be too much of a strain. I was not yet in a wheelchair.

A little girl came up to my bench. She thrust a plastic duck into my hands.

'Here! Fo' you!'

'That's very kind of you. What's his name?'

'He's a she, silly. "Mima".'

'Mima? That's a funny name.'

She giggled, placing small hands over her eyes.

'Je-mima. You *are* funny!'

Sweet innocence. She was all of six years old, long fair hair curling down her back. I wondered what life had in store for her.

'You'd better take Jemima for a walk. She wants to look at the trees and watch the birds.'

The girl climbed on to the bench and sat beside me, tiny

feet dangling inches off the ground. She took the duck and clasped it close to her, rocking it.

'When I was a l'il girl Mummy said she would buy me a bike when I grew up. Now I'm grown up she says Santa Claus will bring it fo' Chrisimiss.'

For a moment I felt sick. If I carried out my plans there would be no more Christmases. Not for me. I gazed at her cherubic face, her glowing cheeks, trying to imagine myself all those years ago, probably sitting on this same weather-beaten bench, cosseted by the family nanny and my splendid parents, my only problem being how to build a Meccano bridge, my only worry whether I'd be allowed to stay up for supper with the grown-ups on Sunday night. Sunday afternoon and evening was Nanny's and the cook's day off, and my elder sister (who was dead now) and I were sometimes allowed to prepare the evening meal. Although my parents had been comfortably off and I had a happy childhood, they were very strict and the slightest misbehaviour on my part during the week meant that on Sunday I had to be in bed at seven, as on weekdays.

'Sweet tender youth, what thoughts and dreams are yours!' Your weeks are months, your months are years; but all too soon the years will pass, the dreams will fade, the tender visions wither and recede. Eagerly you will grow into maturity and spread your wings, and memory will not hold the door of childhood.

Memory-hold-the-door! For no reason I remembered John Buchan, later Lord Tweedsmuir, and his autobiography. He had lived an incredibly full life; I would read his book again.

An attractive woman in her late thirties came up.

'I hope she's not being a pest! Diana has no shame at all in speaking to strangers, I dread to think what she'll be when she grows up.'

I stood up and assured the woman that Diana had been no trouble. But now I wanted to retreat from this reality. Talk of the future was already upsetting me, and nostalgia was something I could do without.

Back at the apartment in Eaton Place I felt calmer and

even contented. I was determined to make the next four weeks a lot of fun, both for myself and others. I could bring a little joy into a few people's lives, then quietly and tidily I would take my leave.

I poured out a vodka and filled the tumbler with ice, taking a new delight in watching the glass frost over, savouring the smooth sting of the liquid. From now onwards I would appreciate every tiny incident and enjoy every moment left to me. I regarded the apartment with a fresh look. I had some good pieces of furniture and some antique silver and very old glasses. It would be fun bequeathing these to friends. I did not have a fortune in the bank, I had lived well and expensively, and such profits I had made had been ploughed back into the business. Even so, I could still give some people, like my secretary Aggie, a pleasant surprise.

My final production must be a huge success.

That evening I stayed up late, fired with enthusiasm and vodka, working and plotting out all the loose ends which must be tied up.

Firstly, I had to decide on the method of destruction. At all costs it had to be final and definite. I could imagine nothing more embarrassing than making a hash of it and having to face anxious and well-meaning friends again.

I wrote down some possibilities.

A high building. Definitely out. I can't bear heights and I'd never have the nerve to do it. Besides, I could injure a pedestrian or give some onlooker a heart attack, and I was determined that nobody would suffer from my final act.

Wrist slashing. No go. Too often it failed, and I just wouldn't have the guts to do it; and I hate the sight of blood. I remembered Robert Benchley's remark: 'I couldn't slash my wrists to save my life.'

Drowning. In the bath? I'd heard that the will to live is so strong that it's almost impossible to drown yourself deliberately; when you're unconscious you bob up again. And I really didn't want to be found in the nude. (Now *there's* a kind of nutty pride!)

Poison. But how to obtain it? And what sort of dose? I'd heard of some sort of weed-killer doing the trick, but I recalled one died in agony, so that was out.

A car crash. No, too uncertain, and the horrible possibility of losing limbs or ending up a scarred vegetable. And again, even against a brick wall, it would involve unpleasantness for other people. Besides, I loved my old Bentley, and she deserved a better fate.

It would have to be sleeping-pills. Quiet, easy, and with a certain amount of dignity, lying in bed. During the past year my doctor had prescribed them for me when I had been sleeping badly, but I had taken very few as I abhor pills of any kind. I had at least a bottle and a half in the medicine cupboard. Now I must find out how strong they were and what constituted a fatal dose.

I went to bed and slept like the proverbial log, the best night's rest I'd had in months.

My secretary, Aggie, is no great beauty, but has a great figure and a fantastic pair of legs. I pressed the buzzer on my desk and watched with pleasure as she entered the office, notebook in hand, and strode elegantly across to her dictation chair. She was a fine secretary and a warm person. She had been with me five years, but I knew little about her private life and had never encouraged any intimacy. I remembered the old adage: 'A lay is a lay, but a good secretary is hard to find.'

'Aggie, I want to give you some letters, but they're to be strictly confidential and the copies to go into my private file. Understood?'

'Understood. Mum's the word. What's the score?'

'I've decided not to produce *Misty Horizon* by myself. My balance is a problem, and I don't want to louse up the film because I can't get around so well. I've been in touch with Warners and made a provisional deal with them, so the office won't lose financially. But I don't want anyone to know just yet, or my colleagues will all be screaming that I'm perfectly capable of producing it myself. Okay?'

She shrugged her attractive shoulders.

'I think it's a shame. I don't know how bad your balance is, you're always so cute about it. Is it that serious?'

I looked at her slim ankles and legs encased in black silk tights, momentarily distracted. 'It's bad enough, especially when I travel. It's a difficult film, and I don't think I'm fit enough. Anyway, I'll keep a watching brief over the whole operation.' The last was a white lie. I'd be dead and goneville long before shooting started.

I left the office early as I had a great deal of planning to carry out. I wanted to make out a list of about a dozen friends and colleagues who would benefit in some way by my demise. A crate of Scotch, a basket of goodies from Fortnum and Mason, or an unexpected cheque. Others would receive some of my antique furniture from the apartment. After an hour's thought I had a list of eighteen people.

The front door-bell rang while I was making a cup of coffee. It was the Reverend Peter Smythe-Watson, looking thoroughly disreputable in a T-shirt and faded jeans.

'Hi, man! Thought I'd drop in and see how the rich capitalists live. How's the old balance?'

'Not so good today. Make a joke and I'll fall over laughing.'

He thought I was cute. 'For an old man you're groovy! When are you coming to my church? I've got a great act, worth a tenner in the box any time. You want a toke with that coffee shit?'

I liked Pete immensely. He had dropped in several times, and I still wasn't certain whether his manner was put on for my benefit.

'You really smoke grass?' I asked curiously.

'Not for pleasure. But sometimes it's the only way I can communicate with some of my rougher congregation. They go for all this "Love Jesus" stuff, but the minute you wear a dog collar you've got to prove you're on the scene and one of them. I don't think God objects too much.'

I gave him a cup of coffee and offered him a cigar.

'Man, that's good. Last week I couldn't even afford a packet of smokes.'

'How on earth did you become a clergyman, Pete? More important, how do you *stay* a clergyman? Doesn't your Bishop object to you going around like a hippie?'

'My Bishop's a lovely man. He knows I'm doing more good this way than spouting religion from the pulpit. My parish is at the wrong end of the Fulham Road, and they're a dicey crowd, but I get along fine with them.'

'Where does Smythe-Watson come from?'

'My honourable family. They think I'm aberrant, ready for a shrink. They paid lots of gelt to send me to Harrow. Man, that was a bum scene. Then they wanted me to take over the family estate in Wiltshire. No, sir! I'm no country squire.'

I drew on the cigar and watched blue coils of smoke curl up to the ceiling. 'You must be a busy man, why am I honoured by this visit?'

His calm, dark eyes watched me steadily; he was a man of many facets.

'There's something about you I can't pin down. Since I first saw you, you seem a lot happier. Are things going better for you?'

'So-so. I'm starting a film soon, that keeps me busy.' My reply was cautious. I had noticed that when he was being serious his flippant language dropped away. I had a feeling this young man was highly intelligent and perceptive.

He grinned, getting to his feet.

'Right on, man. Don't let those old blues get you down. Is it a good film? Up for an Oscar?'

'All producers start by hoping to make a film which could win an Oscar! Unfortunately, there are many variables which occur along the line, and the end result is not always what one intended to create in the beginning. No one is parapsychological when it comes to an audience's reaction.'

'The *Psi* factor?' He regarded me with tolerant amusement. I tested him.

'You use it loosely. Literally, *Psi* is only the twenty-second letter of the Greek alphabet.'

This time he laughed delightedly.

'Oh no you don't! It's the twenty-third letter. I did learn a few things, even at Harrow!'

When he left, I swore bitterly at my intolerable imbalance. Life would almost be worth living just to have a friend like Pete.

The days passed quickly, until one day I awoke and realized it was Saturday the 5th – only one week to go! Most of my business arrangements were now complete. I had made the deal with Warner Brothers, and had telephoned both Don Fellino and Del Pardini, informing them of the change in plan, and that I personally would not be producing *Misty Horizon*. I used the star's unavailability as an excuse, and the fact that Warners would have to approve the new artist. No one seemed too unhappy, the vicissitudes of making a film were multitudinous; in time everything would come together and the film would be made.

Curiously enough, it never once occurred to me to cancel my arrangements. I knew that, possibly, at the last moment I would not have the nerve to commit the act, but my intention never wavered. Nevertheless, I kept an open mind; if some miracle was to happen over the next week, some irrefutable reason why I should continue with my half-life, then I might reconsider the situation. But miracles were in short supply.

By casual inquiries, I ascertained that the sleeping pills were reasonably strong; never more than two were to be taken at night. Sometimes I was invited to a friend's house to make up a fourth at bridge. On one of these occasions one of my partners was a doctor, and during a break for sandwiches I steered the conversation round to a recent case in the newspapers where an ageing film actor had been found lying in some woods, near to death, with a bottle of sleeping pills beside him.

'Of course one feels sorry for him,' I remarked casually, 'but if he really meant it, why not do the job properly? Surely he must have known he hadn't taken enough of the pills?'

The doctor grunted in disapproval. 'The human body is remarkably tough. I gather he swallowed around twelve sleeping tablets. It might have been enough if he hadn't been discovered in time. But to do the job properly, unless they're very mild, he'd need to take double that amount.'

So there I had it. Twenty-five pills would be sufficient, and if I took them on Saturday night, it would be Monday morning before anyone found me, a good thirty-six hours. Moreover, I had a full bottle of fifty and about thirty in another bottle. Eighty would be a very safe bet.

I started to make a list of local people to whom I could leave small gifts of money. My gossipy charwoman, who came in three times a week and kept me delightfully informed of the astonishing goings-on in her neighbourhood; the janitor in the basement, a remarkably useless old fellow with the proverbial heart of gold. If he mended a fuse he would black-out the entire building, and once when he had offered to unblock my kitchen sink he had managed, incredibly, to lose the rubber plunger down the pipe; the milkman; the paper-boy; the postman, always cheery; the dustbin men; the jolly driver who delivered my drink from the local wine shop, who was convinced I was a hopeless alcoholic; my garage attendant; and even the lugubrious old man who cleaned my windows once a month, nonchalantly climbing outside and teetering on the stone ledge. We use many services lightly; at least I could reward them in a small way.

The week-end passed quietly. Now I was almost bored; I was reasonably well-prepared and had completed my lists. There was little I still wanted to accomplish. Perhaps the reason for living had already left me; I had a most peaceful feeling, because there was nothing which could worry me any longer. On the Sunday night I had a cheque-signing session, paying off every bill I owed. During the week I would take out some cash from the bank to cover 'mopping up' expenses.

When I awoke on Monday morning I had a brief pang when I realized that a week from today I would be lying in this same bed, dead. I expected my doctor to arrive about 9 a.m. a week hence; he would receive my letter on his breakfast table, according to when the first post was delivered in his district.

My balance that day was especially bad. Twice I nearly fell over when a second's carelessness caused an overbalance. For appearance's sake, I spent several hours in the office, feigning enthusiasm over future projects and generally taking care of the mundane day-to-day problems.

To me that final week passed very slowly. There were no miracles, only harsh reality.

On Friday the 11th I was up and around early, a festive feeling running through me, the adrenalin flowing and a curious light-heartedness making me sing in the bath, an unholy sound at the best of times. Today I was about to have fun.

I didn't start off too well. Reaching up to a top shelf to get a fresh pot of marmalade, I lost my balance and fell against a shelf of pans, pulling most of them to the ground with a shattering clatter. I lay there laughing like a kid, treating my imbalance like a friendly enemy. All right, you bastard, one up to you, but you'd better make the most of it, because you've only got another thirty-six hours to do your worst.

My chauffeur had been ill with 'flu for two days, so I took a taxi instead of the Bentley. I entered Fortnum and Mason, where I had an account, and spent a happy hour ordering food and drink hampers for a few of my closer friends. Some of them I had ignored over the past few months, and in this way I could make my apologies. The imposing gentleman who served me must have thought I had won a lottery or was going barmy. I put his mind at rest by explaining I was going away for some considerable time (why not tell the truth?) and wanted to leave some presents for my friends. He was extremely co-operative and helped me lower my bank balance by over four hundred pounds.

You might say this was a shocking waste of money, but remember I had nobody to whom to leave it, and that evening I intended to write out my 'charitable' cheques. Besides, one only commits suicide once in a lifetime.

Sternly I warned the gentleman that nothing was to be delivered until the following week, preferably not before Tuesday. I detected a note of relief in his assurance; it would give him time to check on my credit.

Next, I walked slowly across to my tailor in Cork Street and asked him for my account up to date. They were a very old and traditional firm who never expected payment under a year, and I felt they were shocked and almost offended by my insistence. Reluctantly one of the partners managed to add it up and I paid by cheque.

'It's really not necessary, sir—'

'But I want to. I'm going away and I don't know my future address.'

'No matter, sir, in due course we can—'

'No, no! I insist upon clearing my account.'

'Have we offended you in any way, sir? Perhaps the cut of your grey herringbone was not to your liking?'

'It was perfect, as always. Just take the bloody cheque, will you please?'

Next, it was a short walk to Il Cacciatore in Dover Street, one of my favourite Italian restaurants. Their antipasta is the best in London, a huge plate of hors d'oeuvre served with oysters and smoked salmon. I left my splendid little waiter a tip which made his eyes boggle.

I had telephoned the office earlier and told them I would not be in until rather late in the afternoon. This would be my most difficult task, mentally saying good-bye, not only to my colleagues and staff, but to the comfortable office itself, where I had suffered so many chaotic problems and felt the joyous thrill of success, and sometimes the heavy gloom of failure.

I sat at my lovely, well-worn Sheraton desk, remembering

many years ago when I had bought it at an auction sale for a mere song. The auctioneer had been aghast at the lack of bidding, but the owner had put no reserve price on it, and he reluctantly had banged his gavel after fruitlessly glaring around the room for another bid. My humidor stood on the edge of the desk, half full of Monte Cristos and Amor di Cuba, and I wondered who would eventually smoke them. Most of the office detested my cigar-smoking habit.

Several of the staff looked in to say good night, have a good week-end, the usual light repartee. It was difficult to keep my voice steady; for the first time I realized the deadline I had set myself. This really *was* good-bye.

Aggie's farewell was the one I dreaded. Fortunately she made it easy. She had given me several letters to sign, and the next thing I knew was her head popping round the door.

'Sorry I have to rush, boss, but it's Friday night and I'm trying to get the early train. Anything else you want?'

I looked at her smiling face, her day's work finished, the exciting week-end ahead. For a moment I felt a great wave of nostalgia, of week-ends in the distant past, that wonderful 'Friday Night Feeling', where Monday is only a day in the distant future.

'Thanks, no, Aggie. Have a good time.'

Something in my voice stopped her. She opened the door a fraction further, her smile fading.

'You feeling all right? Would you like me to call up a taxi?'

Play it cool, there must be no suspicion. 'Good heavens, I'm fine, just a bit tired from doing some shopping today. I'm just finishing up and then I'll have a drink at the Club on the way home. Now, off with you!'

Satisfied, she blew a kiss and closed the door. Dear Aggie; my death would hurt her more than anyone else, but I had left her a large cheque and she was young and resilient.

Abruptly I stood up, then clutched the side of the desk as the sickening vertigo made the walls spin. Without the aid of my stick I weaved in a curving line across to the small bar and poured out a neat whisky. It was six o'clock and time to begin my final evening.

By nine, back at the apartment, I had almost completed my cheque-writing and had sealed most of my 'farewell' letters. These I had kept light and amusing, briefly explaining that it was better to be a dead producer than an alcoholic cripple. I had typed out a long letter to my solicitor, giving various instructions regarding disbursements of money and belongings, a copy of which I was sending to my bank manager. I sent off a cheque to the RSPCA and another to the Cancer Fund; over the years I had watched too many friends die of this disease, and I was thankful that at least I would not go out in agony.

I was becoming hungry and debated whether to cook something for myself or go to a restaurant. I had already decided that my 'last meal' on the following evening would be at Les Ambassadeurs, where I would dine in style. It seemed a pity to waste this evening by eating at home, but the difficulty of entering a restaurant, circumnavigating my way to a table, avoiding chairs and waiters, always afraid of tripping or bumping into something, took away all the pleasure; and there was constantly the fear of actually falling over and the subsequent embarrassment of being thought inebriated by other diners.

However, I was past being embarrassed now. I would eat at my favourite Chinese place and order the most expensive dishes.

The front door-bell rang and hastily I scooped all the letters into a drawer. It might be Josh, although usually he telephoned before coming round. I made my way down the passage and opened the door.

A petite girl in a wet black mackintosh stood there, shaking the rain from her long hair. For a moment I didn't recognize her.

'It's me,' she announced, 'do I look so different?'

Her hair had grown longer since I had last seen her.

'My God, Margaret! It's years since I saw you. Come on in!'

'Am I disturbing you? Finally I found your address, but you're not in the book, so I couldn't phone in advance.'

'No, I was just going out to eat. Will you join me?'

'Thanks, no. I've already had dinner. I just popped in for a few minutes. I heard you'd been ill or something. Are you all right?'

I looked at her with affection. Several years ago I'd been in love with her, and we had had a long and highly satisfying affair. She was bright, intelligent, amusing, and, unfortunately, smothering in her love. Finally she had issued an ultimatum of marriage, which I had rejected. She had abruptly disappeared from my life.

I helped her out of her raincoat while I explained briefly about my balance problem. She looked around the large sitting-room with approval. My finances had improved since our days together; at that time I had been a theatre producer when fees were meagre and royalties abysmal. She looked up at me, her figure as trim as ever, only tiny laughter lines crinkling her eyes to show she was over thirty.

'It's lovely, just lovely,' she exclaimed gleefully, 'you always did have good taste in furniture, even when you couldn't afford it. I am glad to see you've done so well!'

'I've been lucky. It's disgraceful how much you can make out of just one successful film, if you've been careful with your percentages. But, like gambling, you can lose it awfully quickly again. Sit down and have a drink.'

As I poured the drinks I had a curious feeling. Was this the Miracle? Was this girl out of my past the key to my future? If – and it was a big If – she was to come back to me, could her love and companionship nurse me through the years to come? I asked her how she had found my address.

'I do a bit of charity work near where I live. A few hours a week, looking after old ladies, sometimes doing their shopping if it's a rotten day, talking to them or reading to them, that sort of stuff. It's organized by an incredible character called Pete. He knows you well.'

Pete again, my good Samaritan. Certainly he was a great organizer. I handed her a drink and we toasted each other. I loved the way her huge brown eyes seemed to sparkle with life-zest.

'You must be starving! Can I make you something, or are you meeting people?'

I played it cool, mustn't jump to conclusions.

'No hurry, and I had a late lunch. I'm absolutely delighted to see you again, you completely disappeared from my life.'

She made a little moue with her generous mouth.

'It was the best way. I couldn't go on indefinitely as we were, and I knew you were against marriage. Incidentally, are you married now?'

'Yes and no. My wife left me some months ago. All quite amicable, but she likes the bright lights and I've given all that up since I had this operation. It's difficult for me to get around.'

'She sounds like a charming girl. What about the "for better or worse" jazz?'

I shrugged. 'She's very young, still in her twenties. I guess she didn't want to see me become stagnant.'

'But that's what marriage is all about, isn't it? Helping your mate, the rough with the smooth. As long as you're mentally alert, who cares about whether you can rush around?' Her pixie face looked indignant. All my old feelings for her came flooding back. Suddenly I felt marvellous.

She looked at her watch.

'Gracious, I must fly, I said I'd only come in for a minute.' She stood up and slipped into her black raincoat, belting it tightly round her. 'David's always scared Terry will wake up when I'm out; he's terified of babies although he adores them. Will you come and have dinner with us next week? You'll get along famously together, he's very like you in lots of ways.'

The sinking sensation made me feel almost sick. Her words bounced off the walls like an echo chamber, mocking and deriding my false hopes. Somehow I kept smiling.

'That's sweet of you, Margaret. Can I let you know? I'm not sure where I'll be.'

She stood on tiptoe and kissed my cheek. I smelled the familiar Guerlain Mitsouko, and then she was at the door, an absurdly young sprite perched on high-heeled boots, unaware that fate was laughing at me, taunting me to keep my appointment with death.

As the front door closed I stumbled forward, wanting to cry out, shout something which would stop her. Then reason prevailed, and I sat down wearily. She was married with a child, happy and contented, her anxiety for me merely a whiff of nostalgia, a tenuous strand of human kindness.

I wondered what God and Pete were playing at.

5

The sun streamed through the open window and illuminated tiny particles of dust, striking across the bed and filling the room with bright cheerful light. The distant noise of traffic formed a pleasant inconsequential background.

Reluctantly, I walked off the tennis court where I had just soundly beaten my opponent, acknowledging the applause from the spectators, and opened sleepy eyes to blink in the strong sunlight.

It was Saturday the 12th.

S-Day.

I lay motionless for a few minutes, studying the frieze round the ceiling, for the first time noticing the pattern of tiny angels woven into the design. Spidery brown fingers of decay or mould spread out from one corner, and the whole ceiling needed a paint job. It was some small satisfaction to realize this would no longer be my responsibility.

In fact, I felt extraordinarily happy. I had no more worries or problems in this world, I had the day stretching ahead with nothing to do but enjoy myself, and when night came I would quietly take my farewell from mankind. My production was almost complete, and the final curtain would fall softly and gracefully.

Very poetic, I thought benevolently; you'll probably

chicken out at the last minute; it'll be a horrible anti-climax and you'll have to cancel all those goodies from Fortnum and Mason first thing on Monday morning. I stood up carefully and waited for the room to steady, then dressed in a dark blue pinstripe suit, a new one which fitted beautifully and made me look like a prosperous banker. So be it, today I would act like one.

I walked slowly to my local pub, delighting in the warm sun, the sky a vivid blue. Belgravia looks lovely on a bright Saturday morning, people seem more friendly than during the week, the squares are greener and the pavements cleaner. I was actually grinning when I entered the saloon bar.

'Morning, sir, you look very happy today!'

'I am, Tom, I am. It's a beautiful day, as it should be. It calls for a large vodka and lots of tonic, with ice and a slice of lemon. How's that sexy wife of yours?' Tom's awful spouse, in her thirties, affected heavy mascara and thick red lipstick which gave her the appearance of a female vampire.

'Shocking hangover, she has. Bit of a party last night, had to drag her up to bed by her hair. How's the leg today?'

I had long since given up trying to explain there was nothing wrong with my leg, just because I used a stick. I told him it was much better when it didn't rain. I relaxed on to a bar stool, idly realizing this would be the last drink I would ever have in this pub.

Four weeks earlier, I had imagined this last day would be the worst, a kind of relentless doom approaching hour by hour. Now I felt just the opposite: light-hearted, not at all nostalgic, almost looking forward to oblivion. I wondered what it would be like. A sudden panic before the fade-out? Pain? I hoped not. Would I actually feel my heart shudder to a halt?

And what would happen then? A permanent, unending blackness for evermore? I was not an atheist, more an agnostic, which is a coward's way of saying, 'Prove it, and I'll believe it, but don't bother me now.' I didn't believe there was a heaven and a hell (because *where* were they?), but simultaneously I don't believe the soul actually expires; what a shocking waste if one's entire creation is limited to a short Earth-lifetime.

'Same again, sir?'

'May as well. You only live once.'

I thought of my parents and lovely aunts who were now dead, and all the friends I'd had over the years who had died or been killed. More than anything I looked forward to meeting them again, that would be a true heaven. But what of Billy, my prep-school buddy who had been run over when he was ten? Would he still be ten, or a middle-aged man like myself?

Well, I'd soon know all the answers. I hoped.

Still musing over these questions, I took a cab into Mayfair for my last lunch.

Back at the apartment, I lit the paper and logs in the big fireplace, the central pride of my apartment. I seldom used it, even in winter, as the central heating was more than adequate. But I needed something in which to burn some files.

I unlocked the two big drawers in the bottom of my desk and pulled out a mass of sealed cardboard files, meticulously marked by contents and year. Mainly they were private letters or reports which were confidential, matters which I did not wish even my colleagues to see. There were personal letters too, dating back a lengthy period, important to me at the time, now supremely unimportant after all the years had passed.

It took me an hour to burn all the files. My 'Alive' file I looked through carefully, putting aside notes and correspondence which would assist Josh to settle up minor business affairs. When I had finished I regarded the still-glowing ashes in the grate and wondered what priceless pieces of information I had destroyed; it didn't worry me very much.

Next, I sat at my desk and wrote out envelopes to the trades-people and others to whom I was leaving some cash, and shared out the £10 notes I had withdrawn from the bank on Friday. I wrote a short note to Aggie, telling her personally to give the envelopes to the addressees. I enclosed a substantial cheque made out to her and thanked her for her loyalty over the years.

It was time for the news and I switched on the television set. Depressing, as usual. Next week there would probably be another electricity strike, good news for the candlemakers. I was glad such items would no longer affect me.

Back to my desk, reading through the long letter to my solicitor, sealing it up, addressing and stamping it. Then a short note to my doctor, which he would receive early Monday morning. Again apologies, but please come to collect the old body, then ring Josh at the office and give him the news. Suddenly I thought of my charwoman, she had a key and would come in early on Monday. The poor dear would have hysterics. Luckily she was on the telephone, so I rang her and asked her to come on Tuesday instead.

I found the spare key to the front door and included it in the letter to my doctor.

Now it was drinking time. I took my last bottle of Dom Perignon from the fridge, one I'd been keeping for a special occasion. Tonight was as good as any. I would drink half now and the rest later in the evening.

Half an hour passed pleasantly, then I gathered up all the letters to be posted and began walking slowly towards Park Lane and Les Ambassadeurs. I crossed Belgrave Square, the setting sun casting filamentous shadows through the trees. It was a perfect evening and I was glad, somehow, that it had not been a miserable rainy night. This way, the calm sunset was symbolic and peaceful.

I watched the red mail-box at Hyde Park Corner come closer, and now I could feel my heart beating more rapidly. This was the moment of truth. Up to now I could call the whole plan off, and no one would ever be wiser. Once I had posted the letters I was committed, there could be no aborting.

I stood in front of it, the letters in my hand. Through the envelope of the letter to my doctor I could feel the hard shape of the Yale key. The mouth of the mail-box gaped at me, almost challenging, its wide gash ready to swallow up my life.

'Excuse me, sir. May I?'

An elderly man leant past me and posted his letter. I stepped back, waiting for the Miracle to happen, a sign from heaven that would prevent me posting those damning letters.

Nothing happened.

I thrust them all into the evil slit of the mail-box.

Les Ambassadeurs was crowded but I had reserved a small corner table where I could unobtrusively watch the other diners, many of them well-known personalities in the film industry. Most of them I knew either slightly or well, and I had a moment of misgiving after I sat down. I did not want to become involved in shop-talk, and I considered leaving quickly and dining at some restaurant where I was unknown. Then a feeling of bravado came over me. Let them come and gossip, I was about to eat a splendid final meal, and why shouldn't I enjoy it at one of my favourite places?

The food, as always, was superb and impeccably served. A gourmet might not have approved of my choice, but, after all, it was the final gift to my gastronomic buds. I had Beluga caviar with lemon and chopped egg-whites; some transparent-thin smoked salmon with a slice of a fresh lime; a small grilled sole; and the house speciality, shashlik, with creamed turnips. I never eat a sweet, and by then even the superb Stilton couldn't tempt me. I settled for Turkish coffee and a Hine brandy. I'm not a great wine drinker so I kept to Perrier during the meal; it would have been ironic if I drank too much and the sleeping-pills regurgitated!

Happily, I was left reasonably alone. One or two acquaintances waved from other tables, but during the past few months ill-temper and bad manners on my part obviously had strained our relationships. At ten o'clock I paid the bill in cash and very cautiously weaved my way to the foyer. The doorman, an old friend, greeted me.

'Should be another nice day tomorrow. You going into the country, sir?'

'I'm not sure where I'm going, Harry. "The undiscovered territory from whose bourne no traveller returns." '

'Beg pardon, sir?'

'Shakespeare, Harry. You should read it more often. It's good for the soul.'

'Each to his own, sir! Me, I'm taking a smashing bird down to the pub in Reigate. Afterwards, who knows?'

'You're right, who knows? Well, good luck and good hunting!' On such a farcical note ended my last conversation. I gave him a large tip and flagged down a passing taxi.

By eleven I had taken a luxurious bath, a glass of champagne beside me. My mind was relaxed, a pleasant feeling of euphoria enveloping me. Not for a moment did I consider giving up my Production, nor was I trying to put off the ultimate act. But there was no feeling of haste either.

I dried myself and put on clean pyjamas. At least I could go out like a gentleman. I brushed my teeth and carried a glass of water to my bedside, along with the two bottles of sleeping-pills. Then a thought struck me. I would need more water to swallow eighty pills. I returned from the kitchen with an extra jug of cold water.

I turned out all the lights except at my bedside, and climbed between the sheets. For no reason I remembered dear old Bricktops singing 'Miss Otis Regrets She's Unable to Lunch Today'. Miss Otis was about to be hanged for killing her lover. My end would be much less dramatic.

It was almost midnight. Through the open window came sounds of a party breaking up further down the street. Voices calling out and cars starting up. On the Thames, a mournful sleepy hoot sounded faintly from a passing ship. Then all was quiet again.

I undid the cap of one of the bottles and emptied a quantity into the palm of my hand, wondering how quickly they would act. There was no fear now, only a curious relief that the time had come. I thought of the big house in Scotland where I had been born; forty-eight years ago I was a bundle of warm clothes sleeping in a cot, the whole future ahead of me, the good and the bad times yet to come. On the whole, the good times had been in the majority; I had no regrets.

I swallowed the first handful. They went down quite easily and I ladled out another lot.

Damn! I had forgotten to leave instructions that before being cremated I wanted my ears to be bequeathed to a research hospital. Just possibly a post-mortem on them might save some poor bastard in the future having to go through the same misery as myself. Hastily I swallowed the second dose of pills, then wrote rapidly on the pad by the bedside telephone.

So far so good.

A third swallow of the pills, and now the full bottle was more than half empty. I felt comfortably relaxed, but not even drowsy. There was a slight churning in my stomach, but it could have been mild indigestion from the excellent dinner.

A fourth and fifth handful, finishing the first bottle of fifty pills. Hastily now, I started on the second bottle, in case unconsciousness came quickly. Now they were more difficult to get down, and I noticed my hand was shaking slightly.

Four minutes later I had swallowed every pill, I reckoned about eighty. I screwed on the caps of the two bottles, took a long drink of water, and lay back on the bed.

Did I put out my cigar in the bathroom?

I think so. Difficult to concentrate now.

The ceiling seems far away.

I hope they make a good film of *Misty Horizon*.

I think I'm going now . . . very sleepy.

Sorry, Pete . . .

Part Two

There was singing in the distance, too far away for me to hear properly, possibly only a distortion of my ears. I think my eyes were wide open but there was only a pulsating white mist around me, a rather unpleasant sensation because I had no idea where I was, or even who I was. My brain was functioning, but memory kept slipping away like awakening from a dream and trying unsuccessfully to keep it alive.

No awareness of time; the hovering mist could have been there for minutes or hours. I began to panic, I was unable to move or speak, but I knew I was there. I tried to concentrate and remember who I was and what I was doing in this strange place, but the mental images were distorted and flirting with my mind, always just out of reach.

The light grew stronger and I could hear voices now. Garbled, sing-song, like a Japanese play; a Japanese play? What was a Japanese play? With a mighty effort I tried to lift my head to look around. I looked downwards instead and then the voices and the singing seemed to swamp over my senses, for there was nothing below. No body; no Me.

Perhaps I fainted, for there was a long stillness, just the white screen of mist surrounding the me who wasn't there. My brain, or mind, or soul, or Being, continued to function and now I realized I was dead. There was no fear, only a sadness that I had said good-bye to my body, my old friend who had faithfully carried me around for almost fifty years.

The mist seemed to be thinning, and thankfully I began to see traces of earthly possessions. A chair, a bed – my bed! Then suddenly, without any surprise, I saw my body lying on the bed. Somehow it didn't look like me, although I knew it was; now my thoughts were more lucid. Robert Burns's immortal lines came to me, 'O wad some Pow'r the giftie gie us, to see oursels as others see us!' Some Power was doing just that.

It appeared to be daylight. The singing was starting again, but somehow I knew it was not from the world I had left. It was not a tune, just a rising and falling cadence, like the titubation I had experienced after my ear operation. It certainly didn't sound like a heavenly choir, unless they were hopelessly out of tune.

I found I could see around the room. Not too clearly, the mist was now like a fogged window, blurring some areas. Also I could 'see' behind me, and above and below. It was disconcerting, like the eye of a television camera viewing four screens at the same time. I wondered what would happen next, appreciating that although my thoughts were coherent now, I had no feelings; no worry, no anxiety, no regret, just a pleasant acceptance of the situation. I was not even concerned about what would happen, or of the 'future', if there was to be one.

The mist returned, and for want of a better explanation I must have blacked out. I sensed some time had passed, then I was aware of the white mist again, gradually clearing until I realized I was in a different position, nearer the bed and my body, which had not moved. Abruptly I 'heard' a voice, although it seemed to be speaking in a silent void.

'Interesting, isn't it? A kind of limbo, neither here nor there. Technically, you're not quite dead yet. That's why you keep going back, it's what they call an ectoplasm, a projection of the mind outside the body.'

I could see all the room but there was no one there. I tried answering the voice, by thinking the words.

'Can you hear me? Understand me? Who are you?'

The voice answered, lightly. 'I don't "hear" you, but I understand your thoughts, although they fade a bit; that's because you're still connected down there. You're on the bottom layer of unconsciousness, not long to go now before you break away.'

'But who are you?'

'I can't tell you yet. Not until you've broken away. There's plenty of time. You can—'

Abruptly the mist closed in again.

Blankness.

Statement by Dr Wilmer H. Powell, M.D.

On Monday, the 14th of August, I came down to breakfast as usual at 8 a.m. The morning post had already arrived, mainly consisting of medical leaflets and advertising pamphlets. There were two private letters, one hand-written and the other typed. The typed letter had a hard object inside.

After I poured out coffee I opened the typewritten envelope. It was from a patient of mine, a pleasant fellow in the film business. Since a recent operation on his ear he had suffered from giddiness. He enclosed a Yale key and, after apologizing for the inconvenience, requested me to arrange the disposal of his body.

I did not consider the letter a joke in poor taste. He was not that kind of person. I pocketed the key, briefly explained the problem to my wife, and was lucky to find a taxi cruising past my house. I did not take the time to walk down to my garage nearby for my own car.

We made good time through the early traffic, arriving at his apartment in Eaton Place a few minutes later. I hurried into the flat and to the bedroom where I knew he slept. The bedside light was on, and he was lying on his back, either unconscious or dead. Two large bottles, empty, and a jug of water and a glass were on the bedside table.

Quickly I examined him, detecting a faint heartbeat. According to his letter, he had intended taking the sleeping tablets on Saturday night. I was surprised, if this was so, to find him still alive. I dialled the Emergency service, gave my name, and ordered a high-priority ambulance. Then I dialled the Emergency Admission of the nearest hospital and warned them to stand by.

I then used a laryngoscope to pass an endotracheal tube to maintain the airway.

The ambulance arrived eight minutes later. I informed the intern-in-charge of the circumstances and the patient was carried out on a stretcher. Later, I drove to the hospital and spoke to a Dr B. Marshall, who was in charge of the case. The patient was in the Intensive Care Unit and not expected to live.

7

A dim red light.

Humming noise.

Eyes open. Can't focus.

Throat sore. Bloody sore. Hell when I swallow.

Face above me. A nurse. With four eyes and two mouths.

Both mouths smile, then disappear. The red light is dim and depressing. I'm in a high narrow bed.

Alive? But how? What went wrong? How embarrassing.

Then blankness again.

Voices. I open my eyes. Two nurses this time, normal eyes and only one mouth each, both rather attractive. My body aches abominably and my throat is agony. I try to speak, but nothing happens.

'Welcome to Disneyland,' says a soft voice. A hand raises my head and I feel a glass of water against my mouth. I manage two small sips, but the swallowing is painful. My chest feels as if someone's been hitting it with a large mallet.

There's a large clock on the wall which says 10.30. There are no windows in the room, but now the red light seems more restful.

'Lie back and sleep,' the voice says. It seems like a good idea. Eyes closed, I waft away into black space.

When I awoke, feeling slightly better, I saw the clock was at 4.15. Another face above me, older but smiling sympathetically. I manage a few words, but they come out like soggy cornflakes; my tongue feels enormous.

'It's just after four in the morning. Wednesday morning,' the nurse informs me. 'Can you hear me well?'

'Yeth.' It was the best I could do. She nodded, pleased.

'Good for you! Now listen carefully. You are connected to several tubes, so I don't want you to move suddenly. You've been extremely ill, but the worst is over. You'll have a sore throat and a bruised chest for a few days, but there's nothing to worry about. I want you to drink as much liquid as you can, as often as you can. Pints and pints of it. Understand?'

A little nod, words were large and heavy and too much trouble. She put a thermometer in my mouth and took my pulse, reminding me of my nanny of all those years ago. To my vexation, I started to cry, the thermometer slipping out of my mouth. Gently she put it back.

Time passed, the clock registered seven. A young nurse took my blood pressure and temperature again and gave me more water. My right elbow was extremely sore. I found I could speak almost properly.

'My elbow, it's damn' painful.'

'It's a bit raw. You were resting on it when they found you.'

'Where am I?'

'In hospital. You've been here three days. It's Thursday morning.'

'Thursday! The other nurse said it was Wednesday.'

'So it was. Yesterday. You've been completely out again for the last twenty-four hours!'

I felt slightly better now. 'Can I sit up?'

'Yes, if you feel well enough. But take it slowly, you're still attached. I'll help you.'

The effort was enormous. My body still ached all over and my stomach muscles felt as if they'd been kicked by a horse. She put another pillow under my head.

The red light had been replaced by bright neon. I seemed

to be surrounded by machines. One side of the small room had a large pane of glass, through which another nurse peered at me from some kind of control desk. She waved brightly.

So, for some reason, I was still alive. Too early yet to assess my feelings, simply that I felt highly guilty of causing so much trouble. Sudden panic as I recalled stories of overdoses causing brain damage, waking up like a vegetable. I multiplied fifteen by fifteen, it seemed fairly simple; but I wondered if my memory had been impaired. I sipped some water and tried to remember in detail the happenings of the previous week.

So far, so good. I didn't remember the final moment of passing out, but then one never recalls actually going to sleep. I had a hazy notion of looking down on myself in the bed at a certain point, and of talking to someone, and a white mist which annoyingly had kept obscuring everything. The young nurse with blue eyes interrupted me.

'The doctor will be in to see you in a few minutes. You're looking much better than you were yesterday. Would you like some orange juice?'

'Only if it's with vodka.' She giggled and leant over to straighten my pillows, her pert breasts banging my nose. She smelt clean and fresh and young.

'What's your name?' I asked.

'Norma.' She took a chart from the side of the bed. 'How are your eyes? Are they focusing correctly?'

'They're fine, I think. I wish I could swallow! How old are you?'

'None of your business. You seem to be—'

The door to the room swung open and a man in a white medical coat entered. He was quite young although his bushy sideburns were greying. He took the chart from the nurse and studied it.

'Good morning. I'm Dr Payne and I know it's a godawful name to have in this business. I want you to answer a lot of silly questions as rapidly as you can. What is your name, your address, your date of birth, the time on that clock, the colour of my suit. Quickly!'

I did so, without problems. Unexpectedly he smiled, marking the chart. 'Marvellous! You're a very lucky man even to be alive, and apparently unharmed. Now relax and drink plenty of liquids. Dr Marshall will be in to see you shortly.'

He winked at Norma and stalked out, a competent youngster with his life ahead of him. I envied him.

'Who's Dr Marshall?' I asked Norma.

'She was on duty when you were brought in, so she's responsible for your treatment. Dr Payne is her Chief Assistant.'

I was not looking forward to meeting Dr Marshall. The few women doctors I had known were usually stern and extremely tough ladies, and most doctors despise would-be suicides. I could not expect much sympathy from her. The damned tears started coming to my eyes again. Norma brought over a tissue and wiped them.

'Not to worry! It's a normal reaction, you'll find yourself blubbing all the time.'

'What's Dr Marshall like? Do you see much of her?'

'She's great! She stayed on duty for twenty-four hours after you were brought in; she took only an hour or two of sleep in the visitors' room next door. She saved your life about six times over, she just wasn't going to let you die.'

Hey-ho, I thought, she's just going to love me, wasting her time like that.

There was an abrupt thud on the swing doors and something out of a science-fiction film trundled in.

It was a huge X-ray machine on wheels, driven by an efficient-looking girl technician. She manoeuvred the rubber wheels until the camera, on the end of a heavy boom, was poised over me like a metallic bird of prey.

'Lie still, please,' she commanded. 'You won't feel anything, but it's essential you stay motionless.'

I lay petrified while the eye came nearer until it was almost touching my head. Norma pulled down the bedclothes and I realized I was in the nude. Despite my predicament I was glad to see I had lost a few pounds of unnecessary fat around my waist; over the past year too much drinking and no tennis or golf had taken its inevitable toll.

The girl sitting on the machine was quick and efficient, and extremely bored. I imagine she spent her day rolling along on the big machine throughout the hospital, snapping her pictures like a beach photographer at Brighton, totally uninterested in her subject. Without a word she completed her task and steered the electrically-powered crane out of the door. The second nurse came out of the control room with a jug and glass.

'Time for some more liquid. It's orange, very good for you. We're going off-duty, we'll see you tonight.' A few minutes later a sister in a smart dark blue uniform and a nurse took over.

The sister was young, tough, and black; neat and gentle in her movements. She fluffed up my pillows and asked how we were today. We said we were fine, thanks. We were then forced to drink some more orange juice. Each time I did so, the amount was carefully measured and entered on my chart.

I was still woozy, and must have dozed off. Suddenly I felt a hand on my pulse. I opened my eyes and found a most attractive girl holding my hand.

'Hi!' she said brightly. 'I'm Dr Marshall; I see you're finally with us this morning!'

She was quite lovely, trim in a white blouse and tweed skirt, a short medical jacket worn casually on slim shoulders. She could not have been more than twenty-eight. My sense of humour was not at its best.

'If this is heaven, I take back all I said. I was sure you'd be fat and fifty. Are you doing anything for dinner tonight?'

Her laugh was the silvery tinkle of a waterfall.

'Nothing. Where would you like to go? How about caviar and half a lobster at Scott's?'

Suddenly I felt sick. The thought of food was nauseous.

She studied my chart as she smiled again, a shade sadistically.

'Not so hot, eh? Just stick to liquids for a few days, you won't have any appetite for some time.' She turned and gave some rapid instructions to the black sister, then came back to sit on the bed.

'Let me give you a run-down. Medically, you have little right to be alive. You were brought in here last Monday morning by your own doctor. You apparently had been unconscious for about thirty-two hours. How many pills did you take?'

'About eighty.'

'Incredible. Nothing else?'

'Like what?'

'Just the pills? No other liquids?'

'A few drinks before. Champagne, brandy—'

'You had a large dinner?'

'Yes. It was quite magnificent.'

She smiled dryly. 'Yes, that's what saved you. You're lucky to have a slow digestion, your body was at room temperature, and you were lying down.'

'You make me feel like a bottle of rare wine.'

'You're also fortunate to have a very strong heart, and your blood is excellent. I hope you're a blood donor.'

'I went once. And I fainted.'

'So. We'll move you to a ward tomorrow, you'll be there for about two weeks. The poison's still heavily in your system, you'll have a few ups and downs, but I think the worst is over. How do you feel about it all?'

It was a difficult question. Presumably my balance was as bad as ever; nothing had been solved. I was back at square one with the added embarrassment of facing the world as an unsuccessful suicide.

'I don't know, to be truthful. I *meant* to commit suicide, I can't stand the thought of becoming a helpless cripple. I suppose I should thank you for saving me, but I really didn't want to go on living.'

She patted my hand. 'You know, even cripples can be useful in life. Why are you so sure you'd be one?'

I explained the last specialist's verdict. I tried to give my practical reasons for ending my life. It sounded thin and I was angry that I couldn't defend myself better. She listened carefully, occasionally nodding.

'To me, it makes some sense. But suicide is never the answer unless you're a complete moral coward. Would you try it again when you get out of here?'

'No. Never. I think I can promise that.'

'That's a good start, anyway. What *is* depressing is to save someone's life, nurse them back to health, and know damn well the moment they get discharged they'll try it again. We had a patient upstairs, only about twenty-five, who's been in five times.'

'He's either not serious or not really trying,' I joked, scarcely believing her. 'D'you deal with many suicides?'

Her face became serious. 'Far too many. The ward you're going to is known as The Graveyard. Unofficially, of course. It has twelve beds and it's always full. Almost all are would-be suicides. I'm telling you this because I think you *are* different, and able to cope with your problems.'

I didn't like the idea of the ward at all. Uneasily I asked her: 'I know it sounds a bit snobbish, but I could afford to pay for a private room; I'd prefer that.'

'No chance! First of all, this hospital no longer has private rooms, and secondly, it's going to do you a power of good, whether you like it or not, to spend some time in The Graveyard.'

With that ominous threat she rose to her feet, the lovely face lighting up with a smile. 'So. You'll find you're still very weak, and you won't need any food for some days; we're taking care of that with I.V. tubes and injections. You have a catheter and bag attached to your penis which we'll remove tomorrow, then you can urinate in a bottle, which must be carefully measured. Drink as much as you can. You won't need to defecate for about a week, until you have some solid food, so don't get worried about it. You have a bad scar on one cheek of your bottom; you were resting slightly on one side and the skin tissues there had started to break down with the pressure after so many hours. Ditto with your right elbow, and the same on the top of your right foot, where you had crossed your feet. All these will heal, but they'll take time. Just be thankful you had a bath and your skin was very clean, otherwise you'd have some really nasty scars.'

I listened, humbled and humiliated.

'Why am I still alive? I thought I took about four times the killing dose.'

'You did. You just happen to have superb blood and a very strong heart which refused to give up. Also your undigested gourmet dinner absorbed a great amount of the poison, giving your life span much longer than usual. However, we may still get you into the *Guinness Book of Records*!'

'I appreciate what you've done. I suppose I should say, "thanks for saving my life!" '

'You didn't have any options. But it's nice to hear. Too many suicides realize they're still alive and curse the doctors for interfering. Sadly, they're usually right. Their problems haven't been solved and too often they now have to face life with an additional scar.'

'How d'you mean?'

'You'll see. Some of those patients upstairs are now physically handicapped for the rest of their lives. Some of them have brain damage as well.'

'So I'm lucky, in a way.'

'You're *extremely* lucky. Another hour and even your great heart couldn't have kept going, or you could have been a total idiot, a vegetable. By the time you leave here you'll maybe realize just how insignificant your balance problem is. Enough; I'll pop in tonight and see how you are.'

Shortly after Dr Marshall left, the sister and nurse put on white masks and came to change my dressings. Again I felt the humiliation of being bared and turned over on my stomach, tubes carefully trailing out of my chest and arm, so that the large raw patch on my rear could be swabbed and retaped. Then they gently pulled me round and did the same with my elbow and foot.

I should say that I'm making no attempt to write in medical terms. I know nothing of medicine and I've always resented being ill. I go faint when I see a hypodermic needle, and after my experiences in the war I can't stand the sight of torn flesh or blood. As a layman, all I understood about my 'wounds' was that in the final hours before my doctor arrived my circulation had slowed to such an extent that it was no longer able to feed the skin where pressure was being applied. That is, where my feet were crossed, where I was resting on the right side of my bottom, and my right elbow. Hence the skin had peeled off, leaving raw sores.

I was pushed gently back and propped up by several pillows; my blood pressure, temperature and pulse taken (this was to happen every hour for the next few days) and a large glass of water held threateningly under my nose until reluctantly I drank it.

It was my first real look at the incredible room where I had lain unconscious for so long, where death had come close to being an irrevocable companion, where modern science had fought minute after minute, day after day, to prevent me going over the brink into whatever lay beyond. Strange electrical machines stood ominously beside the bed, their coils and clamps now folded like passive octopodes; red and black rubber tubes twisted and looped up to jars suspended on tripods, gravity causing their contents to seep slowly into my body. Beyond the large glass partition was a desk and chair, behind which was a switchboard reminiscent of Cape Kennedy rocket centre, a mass of dials and switches and multicoloured lights. In a corner stood two heavy oxygen cylinders on rubber-tyred holders.

I began to realize what an Intensive Care Unit really meant; once again I had an overwhelming feeling of guilt; was some unfortunate human, critically injured in an accident, ebbing his life away in the corridor whilst I used up precious space? I felt the tears coming again. The black sister handed me a tissue and answered my question reassuringly.

'We're well equipped with I.C. Units. In an emergency, we could move you out anyway. But we'll keep an eye on you until tomorrow when they take you up to the West Wing. Is there anything you fancy?'

I was still too weak to make the obvious crack as she stood there, slim and efficient in her starched uniform. Instead I croaked: 'Have you a toothbrush? My mouth feels like decayed blotting-paper.'

'What a frightful description!' she remarked, and I wondered where she learnt such accentless English. She returned with an enamel bowl, some toothpaste and a wrapped toothbrush. I tried swallowing a little of the paste to ease my throat, but it still hurt and felt like a lump of raw meat.

The day passed slowly; through most of it I dozed or tried vaguely to plan for the future, but the thoughts were woolly and at times incoherent. At one point I was sure I was in Rome and late for an appointment, and I found the sister holding my feet which I had tried to swing on to the floor. Gently she tucked them in again. Some time later I swallowed two pills with difficulty and felt a needle go into my arm.

Then it was the next day and I faced the unnerving prospect of transferring to The Graveyard.

'The capital of Canada?'

'Ottawa.'

'Twelve times twelve?'

'A hundred and forty-four.'

'Who played Scarlett O'Hara?'

'Vivien Leigh.'

'When did Winston Churchill die?'

'Um, 1966, I think.'

'Good; very good. No sign of amnesia or loss of coherence. How do you feel otherwise?'

Dr Payne was at it again. He had a crumb on one of his sideburns and I wanted to tell him about it, but I was embarrassed and instead waited for it to drop off; it clung with fascinating tenacity. He had very long slim fingers, partly disfigured by dark brown tobacco stains.

'I still ache all over and my throat hurts.'

'I don't mean physically,' he hurrumphed unsympathetically, 'it's your mind and your mentality I'm interested in. Are you sorry you're still alive?'

'I can't answer that yet. As Sam Goldwyn might have said, "I wanted to wake up dead!" I don't imagine any of this has affected my balance or made it any better.'

He nodded, pleased. 'Good thinking; nothing's been

solved and your problem is still there. But you're facing it.'

I wished he wasn't so damned happy about it.

'Of course I'm facing it! Some day soon I've got to walk out of this mausoleum and start life all over again. All I've done is make a fucking ass of myself.'

Now he was delighted. He made some rapid notes on his pad as if I'd announced a perfect cure for hangovers. 'Excellent. You're already taking your responsibilities seriously. It's a pleasure to do business with you!' He must have seen my disgusted look and his smile faded. 'Don't mind my jokes. All too often patients lie there apathetically, barely listening to me, their minds busily working out how next time will be successful. And I know that no matter how I try to help, I'm just wasting my time.'

Now I felt sorry for him; with all his training and brilliance it must be a despairing profession working in a hospital amongst suicides, most of whom had no intention of getting well.

'Have you been here long,' I asked him, 'or do you have to put in a certain amount of time anyway?'

He grimaced. 'A lifetime, it seems. Actually three years. At first I preferred reassuring pregnant mothers that they weren't about to give birth to monsters, but now I've got used to my suicide ward and, despite the frustration, it's much more rewarding. It's a challenge, me against them, and just sometimes I can talk a human being out of trying it again.'

'How about me?'

'You? You're no challenge!' His voice was scornful. 'You're much too sensible and now that you've tried it you'll never do it again.' His beady eyes looked into mine, probing. 'You won't, will you?'

I laughed, and it hurt my chest horribly. 'No, I don't suppose I will. If all those pills didn't work, I'm too much of a coward to try any other way.'

'That's not good enough,' he grumbled, 'there's always a way if you're determined to do it. No, I think you'll face up to your own problems now. Just remember how many people carry on, who are much worse off than you. So you *do* end up in a wheelchair? Bloody lucky in some ways, getting all the attention of a cute dolly to push you around, everyone making way for you, no more standing and queueing. And on top of that, not actually crippled; still able to have some crumpet when you want it. As I say, bloody lucky!'

I knew he was exercising his own psychology, but he made my affliction sound easier. Abruptly he stuffed his notes into a pocket of his white jacket and stood up.

'Okay, lesson's over. I'll be seeing you in the ward. One last thing. In the next few days, look around you, and see what you might have been. Learn by it, but don't let it get you down!' With these ominous words, he strode out.

It was ten o'clock, and I had been sponged over and my dressings changed; blood pressure, temperature and pulse taken for the hundredth time, when the swing doors opened and a stretcher trolley, called a gurney, was wheeled in by a cheery looking attendant. He was old and bald and spoke in a loud Cockney voice.

' 'Allo, sir, 'ere we are, orl ready fer a trip ter Brighton. My name's Fred. Nurse, sweet'eart, yer got 'is papers ready?'

A hefty batch of papers and reports was handed over. The nurses eased me on to the long trolley, transferring two 'drip' bottles on to a metal rod high above my head. I felt a sense of loss leaving the safety of that little room, having to face reality again and to become part of that sinister ward they called The Graveyard. The black sister seemed to read my thoughts. She tucked the sheet round me and stroked my hair.

'Get well soon. Don't forget you're still very weak and everything will seem magnified for the next few days. Small things will upset you, so try not to become too emotional. Just remember every single day you'll get stronger as the poison leaves you. We'll miss you, but it's good to see you go!'

I knew what she meant. Too few patients came out of that room in fair shape; too often they were dead or a hopeless vegetable. I tried to concentrate on how lucky I was supposed to be.

The journey from the Intensive Care Unit to the suicide ward seemed endless. We trundled through long corridors, then took an elevator to the basement. From there Fred wheeled the trolley along a gloomy passage; he explained we were crossing under the main road and into another wing of the hospital.

I was lying flat, and became fascinated by the collection of pipes in the ceiling above me. There were dozens of them, of all sizes. At each intersection a motley collection of them would abruptly wheel off at right angles, whilst others joined the main stream; miles and miles of different pipes, all presumably carrying something somewhere.

Abruptly we came to a wider corridor, flanked on either side by archways leading to huge kitchens and laundry rooms. The noise seemed to crash on top of me, and the sound of trays and cutlery and plates became a cacophony of hell. White-jacketed cooks and attendants moved amongst the stoves and ovens, unconcerned about the crescendo of organized chaos.

'We c'n do over four thousan' meals a day,' shouted Fred proudly. 'The grub's quite good 'ere, not like some 'orspitals I've worked in. You get yer choice, too!'

Now we were in another corridor, quiet and musty, lined with a vast long bookcase, filled with hundreds of big leather volumes. My friendly guide informed me they were the daily records of every patient since the hospital had opened over a hundred years previously. It was an eerie feeling, the red tomes, dark with age, silently holding the secrets of so many battles with disease, won and lost so many years ago. I was glad when we emerged into a modern lobby where Fred signalled for one of the large elevators.

We rode ponderously up to the sixth floor, emerging into a wide, rubber-tiled corridor, bright with daylight. It was the first time I had seen the sky, and I realized that the world outside was still in existence, totally unconcerned about my problems.

At the end of the passage were swing doors. Gently, Fred nudged the trolley through them.

‘ ’Ere you are, sir, safe and sound. ’Ave a good time!’

Suddenly I felt ashamed and afraid. This was The Graveyard, the ward reserved exclusively for members of society who had tried unsuccessfully to kill themselves.

Like myself.

9

The room was huge. Four beds ran down either side, with two beds at each end, making a total of twelve. In the centre, slightly elevated on a large dais, stood a control desk behind which sat two nurses. In front of them were banks of panels and television screens. Beside each bed were complicated electrical machines, to which most of the patients were attached by snaking cables and wires. Above the beds, mounted on long iron grids, were spotlights and cameras. Everywhere there were moving green electronic lines, red and amber warning lights, and rows of flashing white signals. It was reminiscent of an expensive science-fiction film set.

There were two empty beds. I was wheeled across to one of them and gently eased on to it, then my two tubes, still inserted in my arm and my chest, were connected up to glass bottles above the bed. Somehow this very procedure was frightening, a prisoner being shackled into his own particular cell. Now I was one of *them,* a faceless anonymity who would either die or return to the outside world.

After the quietness of the Intensive Care Unit I found the noise overpowering. Apart from the rhythmic hum of the heart machines and computers and the spasmodic bleeps of other unidentified instruments, it reminded me of a cocktail party. Background music was drowned by the noise of talk, laughter, and even shouting. Contrary to my expectations of a gloomy, silent ward, the room seemed to be a very jolly place.

I counted six nurses apart from the two on duty at the control desk. These six seemed to make an endless round of the patients, checking dials, adjusting instruments, taking blood pressures and marking charts, changing dressings or helping a patient walk round the room. It was a bewildering scene of organized action.

A young nurse brought me a large pitcher of orange juice and poured out a glass.

'Four full glasses an hour, please, and no cheating. You can have plain water if you prefer. How are you feeling?'

'Exhausted!' I groaned, and indeed I was. The noise was interminable and very tiring. 'Is it always this loud?'

'You'll get used to it very quickly. We encourage talking as much as possible, it stops patients feeling sorry for themselves, helps them to re-adjust. My name's Gladys, by the way. I'll be taking your pressure and temperature every hour until you're sick of seeing me. Now, let's have a look at your orders!'

I watched as she unhooked my chart from the end of the bed and studied it. She could not have been more than twenty-two, bright and fresh, slightly plump, with a cute face and blonde hair straggily pinned up under the absurd nurse's cap. She could have been one of a million giggly little girls serving behind a shop counter; instead, she was a trained nurse on duty in the ominously named Graveyard, the most mentally unstable ward in the hospital.

She seemed unaware of my scrutiny. 'You seem to be coming along well. There'll be a tea trolley around in a few minutes, try to drink some. You won't feel hungry for several days, so don't attempt to eat. You won't have any bowel movement either, but if you want your bottle, press that bell at the side.'

'What bottle?' I asked stupidly.

'If you want to urinate. Every drop must be measured and

recorded. That's why you must drink as much as you can. Very important.' I felt embarrassed being told about my bodily functions by this young girl. Her face broke into an impish grin. 'Don't look so disapproving, I'm in my third year and I expect you go to the loo like everyone else!'

'Are you always on duty here?' I wanted to be reassured that my new friend would not desert me. I felt alone and unloved, the odd man out in this catatonic jungle.

'Oh, yes. Two weeks on day duty, then one week at night.'

'Don't you hate it in here?'

'Not at all. I volunteered for it months ago. It's much more interesting than the ordinary wards.'

'*Volunteered?* You mean you *prefer* this ward?'

'Sure. Not all healing is confined to the body!' She smiled enigmatically, patted my pillow, and left me. I snuggled down, careful not to disturb the tubes, and closed my eyes. The noise flowed over me and I fell asleep marvelling at the strange quirks of human nature.

The day passed slowly. Apart from having my dressings changed and the interminable black bandage being wrapped round my arm to take my blood pressure, I was given two injections which I suspect made me fairly dopey. I wanted only to sleep, but the continuous noise infiltrated my subconscious like a mediaeval torture, and only minutes seemed to pass before I was being urged to drink more orange juice or to have my temperature taken.

At one point I awoke and found it was evening. The large bright windows had turned to blue-black. With difficulty I sat up, my stomach muscles still aching. Immediately a nurse came over to the bed. I had not seen her previously, and when I looked around I saw only strange faces. 'Where's Gladys?' I asked.

'She's off-duty. We're the night staff. You've had a good sleep. Feel better?'

She was tall and willowy, again in her twenties. I had not yet seen the proverbial fat, middle-aged nurse.

'Are you all out of the chorus line? Where are the stern old biddies who come round with Syrup of Figs?'

She gave me an extra pillow and helped me to sit back. 'Don't worry, we can be just as stern. And we've worse things than Syrup of Figs!'

At some point my wristwatch had been put on the table at my bedside. I saw it was nine o'clock. The talking had diminished, although the constant hum of machinery remained unchanged.

'Dr Marshall was in to see you earlier, but she let you sleep. She'll be in again during the morning.'

Suddenly there was a muted thump – almost a bang – and a red light lit up over the bed opposite me. I noticed the green line on the screen was running flatly across instead of pulsing up and down. Within seconds there were two nurses by the patient's bedside, one with a hypodermic needle and the other bending over the dials and switches. One of the nurses on the control board made several adjustments to her instruments and spoke softly into a microphone.

'What's all that about?' I asked my nurse. She smiled and patted my hand.

'His heart's stopped beating,' she answered casually, but not callously, 'it's the third time today.'

I watched, horrified, as the green spot pulsed straight across the small screen. Even with my very limited knowledge I knew it meant the man was dying, that no heart-beats were being recorded. I felt my own heart thumping in suspense.

Abruptly the green line began to move up and down, irregularly but gradually forming a more rhythmic pattern. The red light winked out; the nurses made some adjustments, then returned to their other chores. I felt a huge wave of relief pass through me.

A sister and a nurse, wheeling a desk-like trolley, stopped at the end of my bed. The sister consulted my chart.

'Good evening! It's pill-time. You feeling a little better tonight?' She whispered something to the nurse, who carefully uncorked some pills and put them in a small container. She came over and handed them to me.

She was quite lovely. Long red hair was firmly pinned in a coil under the cap. Large green eyes, amused, looked down at me.

'Will you take them with water or orange juice?'

God! I thought, it's worth being alive just to see this girl. I stared at her like a star-struck schoolboy. It didn't seem to worry her. She repeated the question, the smile becoming wider.

'I think I need a vodka, please!'

She winked and handed me some water, then returned to her trolley and they moved on to the next patient. My nurse eyed me with amusement. 'That's Rhoda. She's quite a dish, isn't she? All our patients fall in love with her.'

'She's incredible! She could be a top model, even be in films.'

'She was. Then she had to look after her father until he died, and got bitten by the nursing bug. She's one of the nicest girls I've ever met. Come on, take your pills.'

She left me after making sure I had swallowed them. I lay back and watched Rhoda as she moved round the ward. I felt better already.

'Quite a sight, isn't she!' said a voice on my right. The man in the next bed was young, sitting up and reading a book. 'My name's Alec. Been here three weeks; I'm the oldest inhabitant, so to speak. Let me know when you want to talk, and I'll fill you in.'

'Are they all like that?' I asked. 'Even the sisters seem so young.'

'They're a good crowd,' he conceded. 'Some of them are pretty tough, though. We get some weirdo characters in here, who just don't want to lie down.'

'How d'you mean?'

He put down his book. He looked remarkably healthy to me and I wondered how he could have become a would-be suicide.

'Frustration. I've had plenty of opportunity to work it out, both from my point of view and watching others. Lots of people make a half-hearted attempt at it, but it's merely what they call a *cri de coeur*, they don't really mean it, it's only a way of drawing attention to themselves. *They* don't come to this ward. Only the hard cases come here, the ones who really meant to do it properly. So when they wake up, some of them are furious at being saved, angry that they've been forced to return to the world again. On top of it, most of them are suffering pain and injuries and humiliation. Their first reaction is to get out of bed and throw themselves out of the window. I've seen it happen several times.'

'My God, they don't, do they?'

'Not a chance, the windows are shatterproof and they only open six inches. But then they're further frustrated and want to hurt somebody. Usually it's a nurse if there's not a doctor handy.'

I felt sick, hardly able to believe his story. 'You mean they actually attack someone?'

'Oh, not very often. Most cases are well drugged before they're due to wake up, but sometimes the doctors mistime it and the fellow has enough strength to get up. Man, you should see those nurses go into battle, they're like a bloody Commando team!'

'But don't they have male attendants here, who can handle that sort of situation?'

'Yes and no. The hospital is huge and always short-staffed. Some of these poor bitches have to work twelve hours at a stretch instead of the normal eight. They do have attendants and male nurses, but they can't just sit around in this ward on the off-chance someone's going to blow his cork. They get here bloody quick when the alarm's sounded, but the nurses have all been through special training to deal with a maniac case. There's a little one, we call her Bossy Boots – you'll see her tomorrow – who I swear could take on the whole damn Army by herself. I suppose that's one reason why our lovely Florence Nightingales are so young; tackle three healthy girls who know what they're doing and no man has a chance! But you see that black glass window at the end of the room? That's one-way glass, so that anyone in the nurses' rest room behind can see the whole ward; there's usually an intern there as well.'

He picked up his book and flicked over the pages. 'You come in from the I.C.U.?'

I was feeling tired and my brain was not functioning at its best. 'The I.C.U.?'

'The Intensive Care Unit,' he explained patiently.

'Oh. Yes. I was there for several days.'

'Thought so. No sign of fractures or external damage. They bring in some real lulus during the night sometimes, just to die. Too far gone even to try to save. See that guy at the end?'

Up to now I had taken little notice of the other patients. Basically, I felt shy, as their illnesses were no business of mine. I looked at the bed he indicated, noticing the sheet rising over a concave mound. The head seemed to be covered in some white material. I nodded, beginning to wish he would stop talking.

'He'll be gone by morning. He's under a wicker frame, inside a plastic bag. Silly bugger poured a can of petrol over himself, but he didn't die. Yet. He's got no skin and no face, but his heart's still beating. They've shot him full of dope, but it's still a bloody painful way to die.'

My voice was a croak. 'Is there nothing they can do? Surely they have marvellous anti-burn medication now—'

His look was scornful. 'Not a chance, he's way beyond that, there's no way of stopping infection or pneumonia. At least he won't last long. But the guy next to him, *he* has a problem!'

Luckily the bed he indicated was poorly lighted, the overhead spots having been switched off. I could see nothing except the outline of a still figure. Even so, there was something sinister about the very immobility of it.

Alec seemed unconcerned. 'He had a row with his girlfriend, got drunk, and decided to drive his sports car against a brick wall. Hit it at close to a hundred and broke just about everything in his body. If he survives the night, they'll take him up to the theatre tomorrow and start setting the bones.

He'll be in total plaster for months, then they'll try to rebuild his face.'

It sounded like some horror story, which indeed it was. 'His face is smashed as well?'

'Completely. Jaw, nose, the lot. And he's lost his eyes. If he lives, he's going to regret today for the rest of his life. Bloody fool, he was only twenty-five.'

The sheer stupidity of it hit me like a sledgehammer. The polemics of his problem didn't interest me, but only a few hours before that lump of flesh and broken bones had been a young man, his whole life ahead. Now he was faced with unbearable pain and discomfort for months, maybe years, ahead; with blindness as an extra burden. And he himself had caused it!

'How do you know all this?' I whispered, wondering if it was all part of a sick joke Alec was playing on me. After all, he too was a patient, possibly his mind had become warped.

'You just ask the nurses,' he said simply. 'You see, it's part of their therapy. The more you know about what damage you can do to yourself, the less chance there is of you trying it again. Of course, it doesn't always work, sometimes makes the bloke even more determined to do it properly next time. But on the whole it scares a few into giving up the idea.'

Despite the warmth of the ward, I felt cold and clammy. I lay back, trying not to think about those two living corpses lying at the end of the ward, each with a thinking mind screaming to be given release from his mangled body. Alec had said one was past recovery, and perhaps he was the lucky one.

I closed my eyes and tried to sleep, wondering what other shattered bodies and minds surrounded me. The music had been turned off and there were only the distant voices of the nurses and the hum and clicks of machinery, but it seemed like a never-ceasing waterfall, a devil's symphony of creeping terror; a room which had no right to exist but for mankind's own weaknesses.

I heard the loud *thunk* and opened my eyes as the red light flashed on opposite me. The heart screen had a flat green line pulsing across it without a tremor of a bump. The two nurses were already at his bedside. Like the finger of fate the line remained.

After several minutes a senior sister was called over. She listened with a stethoscope, then pulled up the sheet. A nurse turned off the machine and it faded into darkness.

I had never known the man or even seen him, but my pillow was wet with tears.

The boat slid off the rocks and disappeared with a grinding crunch into the crashing seas, leaving me struggling in the black waters and howling wind. The roar of the storm was deafening and I could feel myself being sucked under, suffocating, drowning. I cried out for help and felt a soft hand on my brow.

'There, now. Try turning over a little, you'll sleep better.' It was Rhoda, an angel sent to pluck me from that ghastly maelstrom. She turned me slightly, being careful not to disturb the tubes. But I did not want to return to sleep, dimly I could remember the nightmares parading like evil banshees, dragging me back to some hellish oblivion.

She held out a glass of water. I drank thirstily, my throat painfully accepting the liquid. 'What's the time, please?'

She consulted the fob watch pinned to her starched chest.

'Nearly five. It'll be daylight soon. Will you try to sleep again?'

'I'd rather not. Can I sit up for a little?'

She smiled that rare smile. 'Of course! Thank goodness we don't have any tiresome rules here. I'll get you another pillow.'

When she had helped me up, I looked around the ward with a strange feeling of comfort, my former fears seeming to have vanished. It was warm and friendly, and I watched Rhoda and another nurse slowly circling the room, checking on machines and occasionally comforting a patient who was in pain or awake. There was only one girl on the control board, but I noticed her eyes never left the tell-tale bank of screens in front of her. It was all very reassuring.

To my surprise I saw the heart-beat machine alight on the bed opposite, pulsing strongly. Had I dreamt that the patient had died? I turned slightly and saw Alec was also sitting up. He waved at me.

'Good morning – almost! I like watching the windows slowly light up with the dawn. Did you sleep well?'

'So-so. I think I was having nightmares. Don't you ever sleep?'

'Not much. I had about four hours. I like to know what's going on.'

'It seems quiet. I see that chap across the room is okay again.'

'He's a newcomer, came in about an hour ago. I think he's a fake.'

'The other one . . . died?'

'Oh yes, last night. This one drove up in a taxi to the hospital, with both wrists cut. Can't have been serious.'

I was bewildered. 'Why not? How can you know?'

'Stands to reason. You don't try to commit suicide then get a taxi to the hospital. He's a fake; got scared, I bet.'

The black windows were showing a faint tinge of blue. Very dimly I could make out chimneys and rooftops as London stirred uneasily to another day. I wondered what grief had caused the man opposite to slash his wrists in the middle of the night, then take a cab to the hospital. Why not call an emergency service? Perhaps he had no telephone.

'Old Cinders cooled it,' said my next-bed source of information, 'he screamed a bit till they gave him something. They took him away just a few minutes ago.'

I saw the bed with the wicker frame was flat and empty. Then my heart thudded as I realized what the peculiar smell was in the air. It was like roast pork.

'That smell – is it—?'

He nodded. 'Yes. It's one of the reasons they put them into plastic sacks when they can't do anything, it keeps down the stink of burnt flesh. Actually, they've got the air-conditioning on at full blast now, it'll disappear in a few minutes.'

Now I could hear a distinct low hum, half drowned by the

usual whirr and clicks of the other machinery. Alec continued matter-of-factly: 'You can always tell when they're bringing in a bad burn case, they switch on the air out-take a few minutes before. I've got quite used to it now.'

I lay there, feeling my legs and body, aware that I could see and hear and speak and breathe, with only the slightest discomfort. I thought of the unbearable agony of that roast human being, waiting those hours to die, and the boy who would never drive his sports car again, or any other car, possibly still unaware that on top of his awful injuries he no longer had eyes. What kind of existence lay ahead of him?

For the first time in years I said a silent prayer of thanks. If God was intending to teach me a lesson He was certainly succeeding.

One of the subtle tortures practised in hospitals is the bizarre custom of awakening patients at six a.m. It is, of course, a practice which makes sense. Before the night staff go off duty they must complete their charts with final blood pressures, temperature and pulse; change dressings and briefly sponge the patients; remake crumpled beds; administer such pills or drugs as ordered, and serve morning tea. By eight o'clock, theoretically, they can hand over a fresh and immaculate ward to the day nurses, who then prepare for the early morning rounds of the various doctors and interns.

None of which makes it any more pleasant if one has had a disturbed night and finally drops off to an exhausted sleep, only to be awoken by the ruthless hand of a dedicated nurse.

That first morning in the ward I was lucky, perhaps because I was a new boy. After Alec's gruesome commentary I had managed to sleep, and it was nearly seven before a fat little black nurse brought me back to reality. Her cheerful smile did little to allay my depression, except that it pulled me out of a nightmare where I was being chased by formless ghouls with no faces.

'You've had a nice sleep and here's a cup of tea! Then we'll make your bed and change your dressings. How are we feeling?'

Her accent was a quaint mixture of North Country and West Indian. I loathe tea but I accepted it churlishly after she had propped me up against the pillows. It was half cold and over-sugared, but dutifully I swallowed it.

The ward was now noisy and bright, as if the dangers and fears of the night had been conquered and a new day of hope stretched ahead. The beds were all occupied, so we had a full house, to use a theatrical term. But five of the twelve beds had occupants who were lying flat and still, encased in their own secret horror, or mercifully unconscious. As usual, Alec was sitting up, reading. I felt only half awake, sluggish; hoping he wouldn't start on more of his clinical observation. I turned away from him and found myself staring into the eyes of an elderly man in the next bed.

'Good morning,' I said weakly, not certain whether one should observe the niceties of society. His beady eyes glared at me and he said nothing. Then his toothless mouth gathered itself together and he spat at me. It plopped on the floor and a spittle of saliva ran down his chin. The shiver of apprehension which passed through me was not helped by his malevolent eyes. A passing nurse wiped up the mess and admonished the man.

'None of that, Mr Perry. You promised you'd behave yourself today. That's very naughty of you and rude.' She smiled at me. 'Don't take any notice, he's in one of his tempers.'

She wiped his mouth and again he tried to spit. She took the tissue and rammed it into his mouth, holding it there. Gradually he calmed down and sank back on the pillow. She removed the paper cleaner and patted him on the head.

Not once had his hands appeared from under the sheet. Now she pulled it back and began untying some tapes, and I realized his arms were restrained inside a kind of thick cotton smock. Before releasing him from this she took a black leather strap and carefully fixed it round his neck, then attached it to a device on the top rail of the bed. There was about three feet of slack. She removed the smock and his arms came out like two snakes to claw at the strap, but his hands were encased in what looked like boxing gloves, taped round the wrists, but with no thumbs. The nurse patted him again gently and tucked the sheet in round him. She turned back to me.

'Mr Perry's not very sociable. He tries to tear everything up or attack people with his cutlery, so now we have to feed him ourselves; but he's getting better. Aren't you, Mr Perry?'

Mr Perry lunged forward until the strap tightened round his neck. Obviously he was accustomed to this, because he made no further effort to struggle, but I disliked the ferocious look in his eyes. As the nurse departed he lay back mumbling, making futile attempts to undo the strap with his gloved mitts.

Sickened, I turned back to Alec. 'What happened to him? Is he dangerous?'

Alec gave an airy shrug. 'Sometimes. He's been here almost as long as me. Tried to throw himself under a train, says his married daughter turned him out of the house; he hates the whole world, wants to destroy everything he can get his hands on. Quite a nut case.'

'But can't he strangle himself with that strap round his neck?'

'No, it can't tighten up. But he's learnt not to try to get out of bed. We had an awful time with him the first day, he shot out of bed and tore up five charts and tried to smash up some of the machines before they got to him. Now he's fairly quiet.'

'Good morning!' a voice said. 'Can I get you anything? Breakfast will be here very shortly. My name's Fenchurch. Here's the lunch and dinner menu.'

A good-looking man in his early fifties stood beside my bed. He had a small silvery moustache and a kind, dignified face. He wore a red dressing-gown with pink silk pyjamas underneath. He could have come directly out of a Noël Coward play. Alec called across to him.

'Derek, you owe me four cigarettes again. That's the third night in succession they've given me the wrong order.' To me he explained: 'It doesn't matter what choice of menu you make, they never get it right. I think old Fenchurch here can't spell or else he's paid by the kitchen to take all the left-overs.'

'Absolute nonsense! I can't help it if they make the occasional mistake. They have a lot of people to feed. Take no notice of Alec, dear sir, just you order what you want!' He stood poised with a pad and pen like a gracious maître d'hôtel.

Food was anathema to me. I handed back the menu and explained I was not allowed to eat for several days. He nodded understandingly. 'I should have known; one of *those.* Can I bring you a cup of tea? I'm in charge of the trolley this week.'

I declined with thanks and he wandered away. Alec made a two-fingered sign after him.

'Silly twit! But he's useful to run errands. He's physically well and allowed down to the library; he can get you a morning paper if you want.'

I was puzzled by the man's appearance. 'He's a patient? In here?'

We were interrupted by two cleaning women who advanced into the ward with polishing machines running at full blast. Totally oblivious of the shattered remnants of humanity which lay in the beds, they conscientiously covered the entire shining floor of the room. A third woman came in with a large refuse trolley and emptied the metal bins and baskets. The noise was deafening and I pitied the patients who were seriously ill.

When they were finished, Alec continued.

'Mr Fenchurch is waiting to be transferred to Broadmoor. He killed his wife and two young daughters, then stuck a breadknife in himself. They brought him in with the knife still sticking out of his tummy like a wooden prick. I'll be sorry when he leaves, he's the only one who can make a decent cup of tea.'

'But *why*? Why did he kill them?'

'Says he has no idea, doesn't remember a thing.'

I watched Mr Fenchurch at another patient's bedside, carefully noting down the man's choice for lunch. I had seldom seen a more sane-looking person.

The day staff started to take over; there appeared to be three overlapping shifts, as some nurses did not come on duty until midday or later. My friend Gladys came bustling over with a fresh jug of orange juice. Earlier, another nurse had refilled my water jug; I felt I would drown in liquids.

'My, you're looking better; they tell me you slept well.'

'Yes and no,' I said grumpily, 'there's so much noise all the time it's like Piccadilly Circus. Please could I have a bottle, otherwise I'll burst!'

In a moment she returned with one of those revolting-looking bottles with a flat side. I have always had a horror of bedpans and bottles ever since years previously when I was in hospital to have my appendix out. I was lying uncomfortably on a bedpan, highly painful after such an operation, when a visitor came in unannounced. I was so embarrassed I lay on the damn thing for twenty minutes before she left.

With infinite relief I urinated into the bottle, recalling Darbruck's doubtful, but very true, observation that there was nothing more blissful in life than relieving oneself in an emergency.

Most of the nurses were busy, so I did not ring my bell for attention. Attached to the side of each bed was a metal container into which the bottle fitted upright. I covered it with the cloth and eased it into the container; or so I thought. When I let go, the bottle fell with a crash to the floor, shattering with a loud explosion.

For a moment the hum of machines was the only sound in the ward. Conversation ceased. All capable eyes turned in my direction. Innocently I stared up at the ceiling, wondering if I would be discharged immediately in disgrace. A nurse hurried across with a pail and mop. The babble of talk resumed.

'My!' she said lightly. 'You've flooded half the ward.

Would you be drunk or something? And how am I to measure it in your chart?' Her soft Irish accent was unscolding. I tried to apologize but she was not upset. 'Poor man, don't fret yourself, it happens all the time. I'm thinking it's better to ring for a nurse!'

An army of women in white smocks brought in trays of breakfast. I waved mine away, feeling an odd man out, but totally without any appetite. I felt abysmally tired and weak, and with difficulty slid lower in the bed and tried to sleep. I must have dozed, as the breakfast trays had all disappeared when I opened my eyes and looked around.

The young man in the car crash was no longer in his bed, and I remembered they were taking him to the theatre to start the long process of putting him together. Several doctors were now making their rounds, attended by a senior sister, two nurses and a gaggle of watchful interns. A group moved from Alec's bedside to mine. A large portly doctor led them, his white coat flapping open revealing a silk waistcoat and expensive gold chain.

'Good morning, good morning! And what have we here?' He consulted the chart at the end of my bed. 'Ah, yes, most interesting!' He switched into medical gobbledegook, lecturing his flock as if describing the habits of a leprous guinea-pig. He turned back to me.

'It's your bottom, sir, we're interested in. Nurse, be kind enough to roll the patient over and take off the dressing.'

Before I could protest, the girl had whipped down my sheet and gently but firmly rolled me on to my stomach. I flinched as the dressing was pulled off, but worse was the humiliation of having my arse exposed to those prying bastards. From what little I understood he was explaining that I had lain for about thirty-three hours on the right cheek of my bottom and the skin tissues had started to break down. The drip tube inserted in my chest hurt and I was thoroughly miserable. With relief I felt the dressing being replaced and the nurse pulling me right way up. I cowered under the sheet as the party moved on to the old man next door.

Their stop-over was cursory; Mr Perry's illness was mental, not physical. The doctor spoke briefly and cheerily to him. The little man waved his boxing gloves in the air and lay glowering at the group. They moved on to the next patient.

I became aware of a commotion further up the ward. A doctor and two nurses were working hastily but calmly on the inmate two beds from me. Another nurse was wheeling a large oxygen cylinder to the bedside. I heard sharp, quiet orders being given, and an oxygen mask was applied to the patient. After a minute the doctor applied his stethoscope to the heart, then straightened up. The mask was removed and the sheet pulled up over the head. A nurse pulled bright yellow curtains round the bed. The doctor emerged and walked tiredly over to the control desk. Alec looked over at me.

'Pity. I liked him. Thought he was getting better. Must try and get that book he was reading.'

Five minutes later two attendants entered with a gurney and disappeared behind the curtains. I watched as they emerged with the white-sheeted body and silently left the ward. A nurse wheeled away the oxygen cylinder, and in ten minutes the curtains were pulled back revealing the crisp, freshly-made bed. The bedside table was cleared and the tubes and wires of the machines neatly coiled and in place to receive the next guest.

I was glad to see Dr Marshall enter the ward. She looked her usual elegant self, sleek dark hair falling to her shoulders, a short white jacket half open, showing a pale blue cashmere sweater underneath. She greeted me warmly while she studied my chart.

'H'm, seems all right. Any bad effects from your pills last night?'

'No, except I feel very weak at times.'

'You will. You've still got some poison there. Your scars not too sore?'

'Just uncomfortable. Otherwise fine. I still can't swallow properly.'

'It'll pass. We'll do a blood sample today, and later I'll give you an examination for reflexes. Is the ward depressing you?'

'No,' I answered truthfully, 'I'm a bit shocked but there's something very reassuring about it; it's difficult to explain, but I'm beginning to see what they mean about human life being a sacred pinnacle. What surprises me is that everyone *cares* so much about these people who have tried to throw away their lives.'

'In a way it's more of a challenge to us than an everyday accident case or a normal illness. Anyone who has the desperation to inflict a nearly-fatal wound on himself needs the finest help, both physically and mentally. We try to supply both. I'll be back later. Be good!'

'Before you go, tell me what those cameras are for above each bed.'

She smiled. 'Closed circuit television, wired up to the control desk in such a way that they trigger an alarm if a patient tries to get out of bed if he's not supposed to. The nurse on duty can also switch on the picture and have a close up of any patient at any time. Big Brother is watching you!'

I pondered on this after she left. The precautions seemed almost unnecessary, but certainly nobody would be able to make a move without it being monitored. Shortly I was to see just how necessary these safeguards were.

The patient opposite me, who had taken a taxi to the hospital during the night, was sitting up and being examined by a doctor. He was a small red-faced man with a strong Scottish accent. His wrists were heavily bandaged and he seemed to be in an argumentative mood.

'I'm no' goin', I tell ye! I'm a sick man an' it may be weeks afore I get better. Ye'd no' turn a puir laddie into the streets, would ye?'

The doctor gave a resigned sigh. 'You're about as sick as I am, Jock! Those scratches on your wrists caused a lot of impressive-looking blood, but little else. We can't keep you here!'

Jock held up his wrists imploringly, his face a caricature of pathetic indignation.

'I'm dying, I tell ye, bleedin' to death, an' ye'd turn a mon oot into the snow.'

'It's August and it's a lovely day. Now why d'you want to stay here in a hospital?'

'I hate London, mon, it's so unfriendly. Canna no' gae back to Glasgow?'

'Of course you can. Have you any relatives?'

'Nah. Nae one, an' I havna any pennies. I havna even enough tae buy a wee drappie Scotch. Dinna turn me oot!'

'I'll have a word with our Social Services Department, maybe they can pay your fare to Glasgow. They've already paid for the taxi which brought you here!'

Jock laughed, a dry coughing chuckle.

'Aye, I had a wee bit o' fun wi' the driver. When he saw ma bloody hands he nearly fainted.'

Despite the fact it was almost a comedy sequence, in my weak state I felt desperately sorry for the man and I found myself in tears again. Could anything be more tragic than a man actually slashing his wrists, even though lightly, in order to get into hospital to have company?

My thoughts were interrupted by Gladys arriving to take my temperature and blood pressure. I felt too depressed to make our usual jokes; she noticed this and frowned slightly when she examined the thermometer. I had a feeling it was above normal as I felt unusually hot. She squeezed my hand reassuringly, cheerful as ever.

'Try to sleep for a little, you'll have your ups and downs for a day or two. Oh-oh, here comes Freud!'

It was Dr Payne, who had visited me in the I.C. Unit. He waved to me but pulled up a chair beside the old man next to me. I lay back and listened to the conversation.

'Right, Mr Perry, we're going to start again where we left off. Will you behave if I take off your gloves?'

Mr Perry glared at him, then nodded. The psychiatrist undid the laces and pulled off the padded mitts. The old man flexed his gnarled hands as if they were claws about to strike.

'Now. Listen very carefully, Mr Perry. You are a senior

citizen, a respected member of Society. You have lived a comfortable and fruitful life up to now. Why are you making things so difficult for yourself?'

There was no answer. Dr Payne leant forward and deliberately shouted at his patient. 'Answer me, Mr Perry, or I'll slap your face!'

'Go away! Let me alone,' the old man mouthed. 'I hate you all.'

The doctor sat back. 'Why, Mr Perry?' he said quietly, sympathetically now. 'Why should you hate any of these people? They want to help you.'

It remined me of a tamer with his lion. The old man was vicious but afraid, reluctantly talking only when he wanted to hurt his inquisitor.

'Then let me up. Let me out of this place. I'm all right if you'd just leave me alone.'

'I believed you at first, Mr Perry, but when I let you get up you smashed everything you could lay your hands on. You even tried to stab a nurse with a fork. That's not very friendly, is it? Would you do that now if I let you up?'

'Yes!' he said venemously. 'You're all against me. My own daughter and her fucking husband turned me out too. Why can't you let me be?'

'Not until you can behave like a human being again. If you leave here, would you try to throw yourself in front of a train again? Well?'

Mr Perry maintained a resolute silence. I was too tired to listen further. Dr Payne seemed to be up against a stone wall.

A pleasant young intern stopped by the end of the bed and consulted my chart. 'I'm Dr Dracula,' he grinned. 'I've come for some blood.' He wasn't joking. Expertly, he bound my untubed arm with a tourniquet, found a vein, and withdrew a large syringeful. He sealed it in a container and marked it carefully, made a notation in my chart, and departed.

Then a curious thing occurred. The ward became bigger and the control board receded until it was far away. The noises were louder, like an echo-chamber. I saw Gladys coming towards the bed, but she was in the distance, like looking through the wrong end of a telescope.

It was very disconcerting. I wanted to tell her about *Misty Horizon,* how we were shooting the death scene in Venice, but she wouldn't listen. There had been a hold-up getting the camera steady on a gondola, and one of the crew had been badly burnt when he fell off the roof of the Gritti Palace Hotel. Damn! It was time to get up, Josh would be waiting in the studio car outside, I had slept in. Mustn't arrive late, it sets a bad example . . .

Why is everyone staring down at me? Mind your own business. Jerky and in slow motion, camera must have run at wrong speed, tell the operator he's—

II

Let me digress for a moment with the aid of hindsight. My relapse apparently was not unexpected. I learnt much later that it was not uncommon in the case of severe poisoning; the system makes a final effort to restore itself to normal, and sometimes causes blackouts or a period of hallucinations.

What they did not expect was the total collapse of my system. They had not actually believed I had taken eighty pills, nor had they believed I had been unconscious for thirty-three hours before being brought into the hospital. Their estimate had been about thirty pills, taken on the Sunday night, with a lapse of eight to ten hours before being discovered. It was only because I had extraordinarily good blood and a very strong heart that I had survived; the fact that I had eaten a full dinner, undigested, and taken a bath just before the event, had also helped. The slightest dirt on the skin would have caused a major breakdown of the cellular structure.

Fifteen minutes after I became unconscious I was officially dead. The heart stopped for almost a minute. But thanks to modern science and the speed with which the doctor and nurses worked, it eventually started to beat again. Meanwhile I was in a world of my own.

The boy was twelve years old and afraid. He hated rugger and he trotted on to the field with the rest of his team, feeling the cold air bite through the royal blue jersey. He was skinny and had knobbly knees at which Slater, the thirteen-year-old bully of the class, constantly jeered. There was a blister on his heel, which the heavy boots would rub against and break.

The Sports Master blew his whistle and the boy reluctantly took his place in the scrum. Heads down, arms round their fellow players, most of the team thought it fun to try a quick grope or talk dirty. The boy hated it, even the proximity of their bodies and the smell of sweat sickened him. The scrum broke and almost by mistake he found himself running with the ball. Ahead of him a boy from the other team loomed towards him, grinning, big and tough and intent on pulverizing him.

'Pass! Pass! You twit!' came a cry from an exasperated teammate, but the boy ran on towards his nemesis, his breath choking, fear washing through him. They met with a stunning crash, the charging giant's shoulder ploughing into the boy's thigh in a running tackle. He heard the crack of bone as he hit the almost-frozen ground.

The mist swirled and the boy was eighteen, still afraid, but for other reasons. The girl climbed out of the ancient Austin and indicated the door of a mews house, shabby and unpainted. He followed her upstairs, his heart beating madly, wondering if he could turn and run. The two whiskies were wearing off, the courage he had been summoning for weeks was dissipating. He wished he was home in bed.

The room was cheap and smelled faintly of cooked cabbage. A double bed occupied most of the small room. She took off her shabby raincoat and started to undo her skirt, then held out her hand. Embarrassed, he gave her the money which she dropped into a pot on the mantelpiece. Now she was all smiles and undid her blouse which he saw had a dirty collar. He took one look at the sagging breasts then rushed out of the door and down the stairs.

Out of the mist the old film director, still strong and tall, gazed kindly at the twenty-five-year-old boy who had been listening, enraptured, for the past hour as the director recounted some of the tales of early Hollywood. The boy was his assistant, young and enthusiastic, but a shy gazelle in the film jungle.

'It's time for bed for old 'uns like me,' the director said gently. 'You'll go a long way, son, in this business, because you're smart and have imagination. But you've got to fight for it, every inch, because nobody's going to do it for you, and every step you take up the ladder means there's another twenty wolves underneath you, waiting for you to slip. You kick 'em, boy, and you kick 'em hard! Don't believe anything those bastards and bitches tell you, it's an arena where you either go up or you go under, you can never stay still. Treat 'em fair, yes. But don't do no favours out of kindness, only if it's going to get you a favour in return, or preferably two favours. If a throat has to be cut, make sure it's the other guy's. But when you've scaled the peaks, be sure you look inwards as well as outwards.'

As the mist parted again he saw her standing by the open window, combing the sunlight through her hair. He was in his forties and he marvelled again that he could have captured this young nymph and made her his own. She was more beautiful than the Madonna, her figure a glorious confluence of graceful curves; her personality and wit sparkled and weaved with devastating radiance. He was very much in love with her.

Snatches of life, a jerky newsreel of events in muted black and white.

A period of darkness, a feeling of floating in a vast cavern where the sides stretched out to infinity, although infinity is only a mortal's way of expressing something the brain cannot encompass. Then the mist again, or a fogging of the mind, a sensation of freedom. The bodiless voice spoke.

'You're crossing over at last. I've been waiting for you.'

I didn't know where I was; if only those damned clouds were clear so that I could see him.

'Crossing over where? Where am I, and who are you?'

'All in good time. We must wait a few more minutes, then I'll guide you.'

Suddenly I saw the ludicrous side of it all. 'Of course! I saw that film too. You're Mr Jordan, alias Claude Rains or James Mason! I'm dead, and you're going to lead me through this damned mist up to Heaven!'

The voice chuckled. 'Not bad! Not quite right but close to it. D'you feel cold or warm?'

'Warm. I think. Certainly not chilly. Why?'

'Then you're still attached. Give it another five minutes then we can get going.'

I was becoming exasperated. It's no fun to be surrounded by a mist-like substance talking to someone you can't see.

'Are you trying to tell me that I'm dead? That we're carrying on this barmy conversation on some sort of astral plane? Because I don't feel dead at all!'

Again the chuckle. 'You've been dead before? You know how it feels, do you? A smart alec!'

To prove to myself I was dreaming I held my hand out in front of my face. To my consternation there was nothing there. I tried to pinch my leg but nothing happened, although I could have sworn I was making the motions. It was an eerie and unpleasant sensation. I had to be dreaming. The thought was reassuring and I played along with it. I'd eventually wake up and find it was time to make coffee and go to the office.

'So prove it,' I said icily to my unseen friend, 'what happens now?'

'You're too impatient. You want to see how you're getting on down there?' Abruptly the mist seemed to clear below me and I saw the hospital bed with a doctor and three nurses bending over the patient. Memory flooded back, but there was no sign of the remainder of the ward. The bed seemed to be floating on top of the white mist.

'That's you down there. Your body, anyway,' the voice murmured. 'I'd say another minute and they'll pronounce you dead. You're only holding on by a thread. Stubborn, aren't you?'

I tried shouting at the figures below, but no one took any notice. I tried to will myself to move down, but to no avail. I panicked.

'Help me, you bastard, let me get down there! I don't like this and I don't want to die!'

'Hey-ho, listen to him! He who decided to end it all! Are you chickening out now? Don't waste my time again, I can't keep on . . .'

His voice grew fainter and the mist closed in again. It was darker now, and I felt I was rushing through space, endless and infinite, in a vacuum where distance did not exist. I heard whispers rarefied as a viper's tongue calling to me, tendrils of sound on the periphery of consciousness. It grew darker and darker and I was crying out with heart sounds of pure anguish . . .

I became aware of the familiar chatter of the ward, the babel of voices mixing with the subdued clamour of the machines like a sound-track out of synchronization. I felt a hand on my pulse and I gripped it fiercely, opening my eyes to make sure my limbs still existed. Gladys eased my fingers off her wrist.

'Hey! It's only me! You're fine now.' She called across to the control desk, and a moment later Dr Marshall appeared and gazed down at me.

'You're a real friend! You gave us quite a scare. How do you feel?'

'Exhausted, but okay I think. What happened?' My dream, or whatever it was, was still fresh in my mind.

'A bit of a relapse. We thought we'd lost you for a few minutes. Will you please stop fooling around and get better?'

'How long was I out?' I inquired curiously. It felt like a few minutes.

She consulted her watch. 'About four hours, but you've been under sedation. I'd like you to sit up, and drink some water.'

Gladys helped me and I lay back against the pillows. I felt remotely detached, as if I was watching this happen to another person, a disinterested spectator of the events surrounding me. A short stout nurse with heavy horn-rimmed glasses came across to the bed.

'Any change in the medication, Dr Marshall?' she asked. 'I'm making up the orders for the night staff.'

Dr Marshall put a cool hand on my head. I liked the touch of it. 'He seems back to normal; no temperature. But no pills tonight, I want to make sure the poison's cleared.'

'I feel awfully weak, is that normal?' I asked her. In my lethargic state I hardly cared, but I had no desire to go through that ectoplasmic experience again.

'It'll pass quickly, you've had a couple of injections which will perk you up in no time. Try to get a good night's sleep, it's the best thing in the world for you—'

'—and drink lots of water!'

'—and drink lots of water!' she repeated, laughing.

After she left I looked around the ward. Dinner was being cleared away and some of the nurses were completing their reports at the long table behind the control desk before going off duty. Two of the beds were empty, including the one occupied by the belligerent Scotsman; I hoped he was on his way back to his beloved Glasgow.

I turned and found Alec watching me.

'You nearly bought it, chum! Caused quite a fuss. Feel better now?'

'Yes, but a bit vague. And exhausted.'

'It's the drugs,' he said knowledgeably, 'I forget the name, but it's like pot, you're there but not quite with it. Helps to keep you relaxed.'

'What happened to the little Scotsman?'

'They're putting him on the night train, they'll pay his fare and give him a fiver. They had to dress him because he flatly refused to go, it was quite funny.'

'And the other empty bed?'

'Discharged. A sullen one, I wouldn't be surprised if he's back. It'll be a busy night tonight.'

'Why?'

'Saturday night. There are nine million humans out there. There'll be quarrels, rows and sadness. A lot of drunkenness, too. The early hours of Sunday is the peak time for suicides. Sometimes they're lined up on trolleys in the corridor, waiting to die.'

I could do without this conversation. 'You're a morbid man, Alec. You don't think much of the human race, do you?'

'Not much. I'd sooner be out of it. What's anyone got to look forward to? Responsibility? Making money? Old age? Keeping up with the Joneses? Nah, you can keep it, mate. Next time I won't make a mistake.'

I was feeling slightly stronger, enough to get irritated by his attitude. 'What's the hell wrong with you? You're still in your twenties, you seem intelligent, you have everything to live for, surely! What do you do in life?'

He grinned, unabashed. 'I was a professional football player. Earned a lot of money and I was damn good. The birds used to fall all over me; yep, that was the good life.'

'So, what are you doing in that bed?'

The smile wavered for a moment and I shall never forget the look of infinite regret that passed briefly over his face. He was silent for a minute, his thoughts in a tortured moment of the past. Then he shrugged.

'Two months ago I was coming home from a match. We had won against a better team, and I suppose I had drunk too much. I took a corner too fast, the car somersaulted, and I ended up in a ploughed field, trapped inside.'

I felt an impending horror, but despite myself I had to ask the question.

'What happened?'

'They had to amputate both feet.'

The black sister, whose name I found was Miss Sims, had completed her nightly pill round, assisted by the delectable Rhoda. On Dr Marshall's instructions I was given no antibiotics or other pills. So I was not feeling sleepy. I watched the big windows slowly darken until only the distant lights of high-rise buildings were visible.

Miss Sims came across to check my chart, then sat on the edge of my bed. I guessed she was around thirty-five, thin and elegant, reminding me of a younger Lena Horne, although much darker. She had high cheekbones and huge black eyes, and incredibly long slim fingers. She walked with the unconscious grace of her ancestors, and she, too, could have made a fortune as a *Vogue* model. There was a comforting aura about her, a sense of discipline and intelligence which one felt could cope with any emergency. I had noticed she commanded instant respect from the nurses, although her tone of voice was always low and pleasant.

'I thought I'd have a quick chat with you while things are quiet,' she said softly, 'I didn't have much chance last night. First of all, I'm happy you're still with us, I gather you had a bad day. You should be all right now, there's rarely a second relapse, and your heart's as good as ever.'

She handed me a glass of orange juice, which I automatically started to sip.

'It's important that you start to live your life again as soon as possible. By that I mean you should get interested in what's going on outside. Get a newspaper tomorrow, try to write a letter or two if you feel well enough; anything to get yourself in contact again.'

I sighed, not relishing the idea. 'I suppose you're right, but I'm going to feel an awful fool having to face everyone again.'

She smiled, her teeth white and even against the ebony. 'So what? You'd be surprised how glad they'll be to see you again. When a suicide succeeds it leaves a lot of people feeling guilty!'

I'd never thought of that. Then I remembered how I had felt some years before when a friend of mine had shot himself. He'd telephoned me one evening and asked me to go round for a drink. I'd been busy and told him to make it sometime the following week. He had rung two other people with the same consequence, and an hour later had put the gun to his head. In his case, his wife had died and his business gone into liquidation. But how are we to know when the real *cri de coeur* comes? I had felt guilty for weeks after.

'In your case, I don't think being in this ward will particularly help you. To some people it's therapeutic, jolts them into reality again, but it can also be highly upsetting. It's possible tonight may be a bit grim, so try to sleep through it and get your strength back. Would a cup of tea help?'

'No. Thanks. With all due respect, the tea here, as the man said, looks like coffee and tastes like cocoa!'

She laughed and stood up. 'Agreed! Let me know when you want your pillows taken away.'

She excused herself as the swing doors opened and a trolley was wheeled in bearing the motionless form of a man. They took him to the bed opposite and I noticed it required the attendant and three nurses to slide him on to the bed, he seemed so enormous. They tucked him in and attached a drip to his arm, then a nurse took his blood pressure and felt his pulse and marked it on a new chart.

The ward was settling down for an uneasy night, and top lights were dimmed. Alec, as usual, was reading by his overhead lamp. Mr Perry seemed to be asleep, his arms presumably held inside the laced sheet. I wondered what disjointed thoughts were running through his mind and whether he would ever recover from his traumatic condition.

The car-crash boy was back on his bed, encased in a mountain of white plaster which precluded me from seeing his face. I hoped he was well drugged, as even when he had climbed his mountain of agony, it would still continue when he reached the summit.

After a while, Rhoda came across to remove two pillows and leave me with my small sleeping pillow.

I wanted to keep her close to me. 'Do I have to go to sleep?'

'Gracious, no! There's no "Lights Out" here. D'you want to read something?'

'No. I'm tired but not sleepy. Just leave another pillow will you? I'll contemplate my navel and think of all the great films I'm going to produce.'

'I made a film once. I had one line and I fluffed it. In front of all those people, it was awful!'

'What happened?'

'I played the maid in a period film. I had to rush in and find the room empty, and say, "Oh my God, they've gone!" '

'That's not too difficult to remember?'

She made a moue with the attractive mouth. 'I was so scared I rushed in and said: "Oh my gone, they've God!" That was the end of my film career.'

There was a *thunk* and a red light from a bed at the end of the ward. Quietly but swiftly she left me to assist another nurse. Alec gave a casual glance at the red light.

'Was expecting that. Doubt if they'll save him, he was pretty far gone.'

Alec was right. In a few minutes the yellow curtains were closed round the bed, the control desk nurse spoke briefly into her microphone, and almost immediately an empty gurney was wheeled in by an orderly. I watched the covered body being taken out and realized that, whoever he was, this was what he had wanted. Death was a welcome friend; worldly problems solved for evermore.

Which brought me round to my dream, or hallucination. Or was it? Both times I had 'floated' – for want of a better description – apparently I had been momentarily dead. I know the heart can continue after the brain is dead, but the brain only lasts a minute or two after the heart stops beating. Does that mean that the brain, or spirit, has actually departed from the body? The second time it had happened I knew I had no physical body, yet I could 'see' and 'hear'. Had I been about to 'pass over' (what a repulsive expression) but each time been pulled back by the heart starting to beat again? Or was it all just subconscious imagination?

I closed my eyes, but could not sleep. The tube in my chest, held in position by strips of sticking plaster, itched and hurt. The noise of the ward beat down and I longed for blessed silence. Somewhere a patient was coughing endlessly, wracking coughs from deep in his chest. A nurse was soothing someone who was crying, I could hear her soft voice and his quiet sobbing, agony and anguish mixed in hopeless abandon. Machines hummed and clicked and whirred like some devilish computer. Someone snored loudly, somehow incongruously domestic in its surroundings.

I became aware of a deeper throbbing sound, and realized it was the air-conditioning unit turned full on. I remembered Alec's words, and waited with a feeling of tenseness for what was about to come.

I had not long to wait. The doors opened silently and the stretcher was wheeled in by two orderlies. The figure was sheeted, but as it passed the foot of my bed I saw a mop of burnt hair and the entire face covered in white foam from which came low animal moans. Gently they lifted it on to the recently vacated bed at the end of the ward, and then there was a piercing shriek which cut through me like a sword, leaving my heart beating madly in sheer fright.

No one else seemed to have been disturbed. The myriad noises continued unabated. A nurse gave the man an injection, while Rhoda connected up a drip tube to his arm. It was all very efficient, and I tried to relax and remember Miss Sims's advice.

Some time later another trolley was wheeled in, and a motionless figure deposited on the last empty bed. He was left alone, no tubes or heart machine attached. At intervals a nurse checked on him. Within an hour the trolley was back and the still figure had departed.

As the hours passed I had a growing feeling of panic. It was impossible to sleep, and the ward was slowly closing in, the sounds becoming louder and more sinister. At some point a red light *thunked* on, and I was dimly aware of another body being taken out. I knew it was my turn next, but I was not connected to the heart machinery and I wondered how they would know when I was dead. Then I saw the evil camera glaring down at me, and I knew it was waiting for me to go, that it had been waiting for forty-nine years, knowing that its moment would come. One of the closed-circuit screens on the control desk would light up, the nurse would make a notation in her log, press a buzzer, and the gurney would come silently in and another bed would be empty and waiting expectantly for the next in the queue.

I heard a shout and opened my eyes. The huge man in the bed opposite was sitting up, pulling off the drip tube and screaming obscenities. Then I knew I was in Hell, that I had died and this was my punishment.

He was a monster, literally. His head was much too small for his body, and completely bald. He had only one eye and there was smooth skin where the other should have been. His nose was long and crooked, like a miniature trunk, and his mouth was a slit with no lips. It was something out of a nightmare.

He swung his legs on to the floor and stood up, a mountain of a man, the small head perched incongruously on top of the massive shoulders. With one sweep of his arm he cleared his bedside table, glasses and a jug crashing to the floor.

There was pandemonium now. A patient started to scream and Mr Perry began to shout. A man called out loudly for Jesus to save him, over and over. A buzzer sounded warningly. The monster strode towards the ward doors.

Miss Sims, Rhoda, and another nurse reached him. Within seconds they had both his arms twisted up behind his back. The nurse pulled a canvas bag over his head. An intern came running from the back of the ward, hypodermic in hand. In a trice it was discharged into the giant's buttock.

His shouting stopped. The nurses turned him round and led him back to the bed. He shook his head groggily and collapsed on his back. The nurse removed the canvas sack and within seconds the intern was slipping the arms into a heavy strait-jacket which he tied by tapes to the sides of the bed. Meanwhile two other nurses were calming the patients, and within a short time the ward resumed its normal tempo.

The windows held the first trace of dawn before I fell into an uneasy sleep.

Sundays were no different in The Graveyard. By eight o'clock the usual procedures had been carried out, the ward cleaned and polished, the patients fed and bathed, and the reports written up. The day staff mingled in gradually as the night nurses left for their well-earned rest. The dramas of the night were phased out by the reality of day.

Provided there were no immediate emergencies, at 8.30 each morning the Floor Matron presided over the sisters and nurses at the long table in the centre of the room. Each patient's chart was examined and discussed, bringing the nurses up to date with the night's casualties and happenings. During this time only one nurse remained at the control centre. We, the patients, were unable to hear what was said, but usually within minutes of the meeting being finished, my friend Alec had all the latest gossip and information.

I felt slightly stronger, but still exhaustingly tired. Mr Fenchurch, the family-killer, came round with a pile of Sunday newspapers. I accepted the *Sunday Telegraph* although the effort of reading was still difficult, my eyes were not focusing properly and the print kept sliding off the pages.

I drank some tea and examined the ward. Mr Perry was in trouble as usual. Gladys had tried to feed him some cornflakes, which he kept spitting over her and the floor. If it wasn't so pathetic it would have been funny. Patiently she spooned them into his mouth, and equally determinedly he sprayed them out over the bed and on to her lap. When he refused to accept a spoonful she smacked him lightly on the face until he opened his mouth.

Beyond Mr Perry the bed was empty, presumably another casualty of the night. Opposite me, the huge figure of King Kong, as Alec was to name him, lay motionless. On his left, an elderly man sat up reading a newspaper, and next to him was an unmade bed belonging to Mr Fenchurch. On my right, beyond Alec's bed, a man lay motionless, jet-black hands folded over his sheet. At the end of the ward lay the burn case, a wicker frame covered with the sheet making it impossible to see his face. The bed next to him contained the plaster-entombed car-crash boy.

A small nurse, on the stout side and wearing glasses, came across to Mr Perry and regarded the mess with disgust. Cornflakes lay on the bed and the floor and Gladys was attempting to clear them up. The little nurse had scant sympathy for him.

'Mr Perry, you are a pain in the arse! If you refuse to eat you're going to get a tube down your throat again, and you remember what a fuss you made last time. I'll give you till lunch-time, and if you don't eat then, you're for the chop.'

She leaned over him and undid his restraining sheet. His thin arms emerged, the bony fingers curved like talons. His rheumy eyes stared into hers, as if wondering whether it was worth while to attack. I had seen the same look on a wild cat, scared and cornered, poised ready to spring on its attacker, but knowing it will suffer afterwards. Surprisingly, the little nurse took one of his hands in hers. Now she spoke softly, coaxingly.

'Come on now, Mr Perry, we're not all villains. Would you like me to rub your back?'

It didn't work. Mr Perry drew back and almost hissed at her, his fingers clenching and unclenching. Alec leaned across and whispered to me.

'That's Miss Bossy Boots. Don't get on the wrong side of her, she can be very ugly when she wants!'

Bossy Boots proved his point. She leaned forward until her face was only a few inches from Mr Perry's. 'All right, old man! You get nasty and I'll get nasty. Now, I'm going to leave off your gloves, but if you tear anything up, or get violent in any way, I'll chain them back on and throw away the key. Understand? Do YOU UNDERSTAND?'

They glared at each other for a full ten seconds, then Mr Perry mumbled something and turned away. Bossy Boots came over to my bed and consulted my chart.

'Well, are you going to be good today, or are we going to have another try-on for the suicide stakes?'

'I'm fine,' I murmured weakly, 'I don't remember much about yesterday, honestly!'

'That's what they all say. Avoiding your responsibilities! There's nothing wrong with you that a little determination won't cure. Drink your orange juice and we'll have you out of here in no time.'

She passed on to Alec's bed; he was made of sterner stuff than me. He believed that the best form of defence was to attack. 'Hi, Bossy Boots, did you get laid last night?'

'None of your lip, young man. Don't think this is some smart Rest Clinic where you can lounge around for ever. Your feet will be here tomorrow and I want to see you walking within a week.'

It sounded cruel in its bare context, but I was beginning to learn that patients had to face up to the truth, that sympathy was taboo, although compassion was always present. Alec was not put out by her abrupt statement.

'Who needs feet? I'd rather lie around, eating your superb caviar, being waited on by you lovely broads. Did I tell you I fucked that nice little West Indian nurse last night?'

I waited for a devastating reply. Instead Bossy Boots giggled girlishly. 'You should be so lucky! Just you be careful or I'll visit you one night and really teach you something!' Alec pulled the sheet over his head in mock horror. She glanced at his chart then carried on to the next patient. It was the black man, now sitting up and reading a paper. I tried to hear what they said.

'Hey-ho, Septimus, how's the throat?'

I noticed his neck was heavily bandaged. The black man, in his forties, grinned at her. 'Mighty fine, sister, I feel kind of a fraud lying here. Can I get up today?'

'No reason why not. Wait until after the geniuses have made their rounds, then I'll help you. Just keep your head steady and mind those stitches, we wouldn't want it to fall off.'

Alec leaned towards me. 'Silly bugger cut his throat with a carving knife, but it wasn't sharp enough. He's a preacher, too, a genuine clergyman. I wonder how he would have explained it away to God!'

'That burn case,' I asked, 'the one that came in during the night, what did he do?'

Alec broke into laughter. 'Incredible, really truth is stranger than fiction. He tried the gas oven lark, lay there for five minutes, then lit a cigarette. Bam! He blew half his face away.'

I found myself listening with interest, no longer appalled at what human beings could do to themselves. I wondered, for every failure, how many were successful. Just how many people actually committed suicide every day? Was modern society so unbearable? I felt *my* effort had had a definite reason, that it made complete sense, then I realized that to each individual, at that crucial moment of committing the act, it made sense to him. It was a sobering thought. We live cocooned in our own small world, bounded by territories of self-interest and greed.

One hundred years ago, and indeed until the 1950s, the cardinal sin was suicide; punishable, if unsuccessful, in law. Now society took a more tolerant view, and I mused on the possibilities of a hundred years hence. Would there be clinics in every town, almost like betting shops, where one could go to be mercifully killed? Why not? With the population increasing out of all proportion and people's longevity improving, why not let the misfits and the failures have the privilege of dying in a dignified manner, at their own request, rather than clutter up much-needed beds and use the valuable time of doctors and nurses as a result of their pathetic and often gory self-attempts? I recalled the superb scene in the film *Soylent Green*, where Edward G. Robinson goes to such a clinic, is duly injected, and lies on a comfortable couch while a panorama of a beautiful sunset is projected above him and his favourite music is piped into the room. How much more civilized than the youth in the ward who drove his car into a brick wall, who might have killed innocent people, and even now, for the rest of his life, would require skilled assistance from another human being; a waste of two lives and endless other people on the periphery of his misery.

Two old ladies entered the ward, wheeling a mobile library, with shelves of sweets and toilet articles. I bought a toothbrush and some toothpaste with money I borrowed from Alec, then I invested in a notebook and pencil; I had to start making plans.

Dr Marshall arrived, apologizing for her non-appearance the previous afternoon to carry out my tests. She was wearing jodhpurs and boots, and a rough green hacking jacket. She would look superb on a horse, although in my eyes she looked superb at any time.

'I had an emergency operation yesterday, a long one. I'll get changed and be back shortly. Did you sleep well?'

'No. There's so much noise, I was awake till about 5.30, but I feel a bit stronger today.'

'Good. I'll see you get a couple of sleeping-pills tonight.' She smiled impishly. 'I know how much you like them!'

She walked over to the burned man, consulted his chart and conferred with Bossy Boots. Then she waved to me and left the ward. I turned to Alec.

'Doesn't she ever have a day off? It's Sunday!'

'She never seems to, comes in sometimes in the middle of the night, sometimes sleeps in the hospital. I like that broad, she's one of the best.' I agreed, deciding that Rhoda and Dr Marshall were now my first loves.

I had hardly looked at the *Sunday Telegraph*, it was an effort to concentrate on the words, and I found myself reading each paragraph several times. I picked up the Supplement and on an impulse leant across and offered it to Mr Perry.

He regarded me suspiciously. 'Would you like to read it, Mr Perry? It's quite interesting this week.' I didn't expect him to take it. To my surprise a bony arm extended and snatched it from me. He lay back and opened it, hastily thumbing through the pages, barely glancing at them. Then he started tearing them. There was something obscene in the way he clawed at each page and ripped it to shreds, scattering the pieces on the bed and floor. A trickle of saliva ran from his mouth and he panted like an animal.

Bossy Boots ran over and wrestled the magazine from him. Without a word she left him and in a moment returned with a nurse and his padded gloves. The nurse held his arms while Bossy Boots slipped on the gloves and laced them tightly. Mr Perry waved his arms in the air and tried to hit the nurse. He leant forward and the strap round his neck tightened and pulled him back.

'It's your own fault, you silly man. Why can't you behave yourself?' She turned to me. 'I'm sorry about your magazine, there's not much left of it. Incidentally, are you ready to receive visitors? We've had several inquiries; up to now we've said you were too ill. How about it?'

I did not want to see anyone, it would be too embarrassing, both for me and the visitor. I told her I'd prefer to wait a day or two.

'All right, but you've got to face them eventually,' she snapped, 'the sooner the better.'

I noticed the yellow curtains had been pulled round Alec's bed, and I presumed his artificial feet had arrived. I could almost sympathize with his suicidal inclination; to have to wear false legs, even from below the knee, must be a traumatic experience; especially for a professional footballer.

Two doctors and two nurses were examining the burn case, one of the medicos bending low over the face with a flashlight and magnifying goggles. A nurse gave an injection.

The second doctor turned to a sister who had just entered the ward. 'Book a theatre for eight a.m., Sister, meanwhile we'll continue the—' A long medical formula followed which I couldn't understand.

At the opposite side of the ward, at the end nearest the swing doors, the patient who had coughed all night was sitting up reading a Sunday newspaper. It was the *News of the World*. He was quite young, with a drawn, sallow face and a long thin nose. He wore bright purple pyjamas with some sort of crest on the breast pocket. He coughed intermittently, a deep harsh sound which racked his body. Each time it happened his face contorted with pain. Gladys had come over to give me the two-hourly blood pressure check, so I boldly asked her what ailed the Coughing Man. Why should Alec have a monopoly on gossip?

She screwed her elfin little face in concentration. She gave the impression of being dumb but I suspected she was a lot more intelligent than she pretended.

'They're not sure yet. He won't say a word, but apparently he swallowed some kind of acid. He's got tuberculosis, and it must be hell for him to cough, his throat's burnt away.'

'Is he seriously ill, then?'

'Yes. He went to the loo during the night and tried to drown himself in the pan. But the Control Sister sent a nurse in when he didn't come out after five minutes. Poor man, he's really very polite and no trouble at all.'

'Who's the man next to him?' I asked curiously. He was in his fifties, with steel spectacles on the end of his nose. He had some sort of contraption round his chest and shoulders. He lay upright against several pillows, his eyes closed.

'Mr Carstairs? He's a darling. His wife left him because he became impotent, and he jumped out of the window of his apartment, eight floors up. At the last moment he thought better of it, and clung on to the balcony rail.'

'He was saved, then?'

'Just. He hung by his hands for nearly ten minutes before being rescued; dislocated both his collar bones. But he's got a weak heart so they're keeping him in for a few more days.'

I noticed he was attached by wires to a heart machine, the green blip of which seemed to be pulsing healthily.

For no good reason, I felt strangely warm and snug as I looked around the ward. Undoubtedly I was the fittest and the luckiest patient there, and I could look with pity and compassion on my fellow inmates. I had a strong desire to help in some way, if only to show some gratitude towards the hospital which had taken me in without anger or recrimination.

I dozed and reminisced in a pleasant warm euphoria, probably brought on by two injections which Bossy Boots gave me. When I asked what they were, she told me to mind my own business. She wasn't my favourite pin-up, but she certainly was efficient. The day passed slowly, and eventually Dr Marshall returned, dressed in a business-like white smock, and proceeded to examine me, literally from toe to head.

She had a small rubber mallet and some sort of sharp needle. She worked up from my feet to my neck, probing and banging and pricking, testing my reflexes and ascertaining whether I had any numb patches of skin. She seemed satisfied that I had reacted satisfactorily. I even had the strength to murmur: 'A small prick can lead to a big bang!' She laughed loudly, but I could see her eyes were rimmed with tiredness; it was a helluva way to spend a Sunday afternoon.

A patient across the ward was being fed soup by one of the nurses. He was a middle-aged man with a red face and an unpleasant, sour expression. He was spitting out the soup and swearing at the nurse in coarse, obscene language. The nurse, unruffled, continued to try to feed him.

'Come along now, you've got to eat something, otherwise you'll lose your strength.'

'Little bitch, I don't want you bloody whores telling me what to do! Why didn't you let me die, what right have you to act like God? Little swine!' The oaths rolled out, his face working crazily and the soup trickling down his chin.

The nurse sighed and put down the bowl. She walked over

to Tessa, the black nurse, and spoke a few words. Tessa nodded, fetched a small towel and returned with the nurse to the patient's bedside. Without a word the nurse put her arms tightly round the man's chest, imprisoning his arms, while Tessa took the folded towel and clamped it over his face, her other hand firmly holding the back of his head. Seconds passed as the patient tried to break away, but the nurses were strong and he was no match for them. He started suffocating, and his body writhed as he fought for air.

I watched, fascinated, as little Tessa kept the towel over his face, at the same time talking casually to the other girl. Eventually she released the man, and he heaved in great gulps of air, coughing and spluttering.

'Now,' said the nurse brightly, 'you will eat your soup and you'll stop that filthy language. Try to behave like a gentleman even if you've never heard the word before. Do you dig me? Understand? Savvy? If you swear once again we'll suffocate you until you're unconscious!'

She ignored the look of rage which he gave her, but he accepted the next spoonful and maintained a discreet silence.

Dinner came and departed. I still had no appetite and I hoped never to see orange juice again. Mr Fenchurch poured me out a cup of weak coffee from his trolley which he proudly wheeled round the ward after each meal.

'You're an unusual fellow,' he remarked, sipping his own cup and ignoring other patients who were waiting for their coffee. 'I can't imagine why you're in here. Would you like to tell me about it? Confidentially, of course.'

The last thing I wanted to do was talk about my problems with a fellow patient. 'No, it's much too complicated, I don't think I want to discuss it.' I tried to make it as kind as possible; he obviously meant well and I had no wish to hurt his feelings. 'May I ask why *you* are here, or shouldn't I? In which case I apologize.'

'My dear fellow, I'm not a patient! No, no. I'm employed here to handle the tea trolley. A good job, too, although they're very stingy with the supplies, that's why the coffee and tea sometimes seem a bit weak. I have to make it go around.'

I looked at this distinguished man, his flowing grey hair and neatly trimmed moustache, the silk pyjamas and expensive dressing-gown, and wondered if he genuinely had retreated into a dream world, or whether it was a pose, an amnesiac protection against the dreadful crime he had committed. His self-inflicted wound seemed to have healed, as he moved normally, although once when I saw him bend down to pick up a teaspoon he clutched his stomach and appeared to be in pain. Later, Alec told me he had been a Chartered Accountant and a director of a top firm of solicitors in the City, and was also a magistrate in his local village in Kent. What tiny stratum of his brain had twisted to turn this respectable man into a killer? I was glad I was not a neurologist faced with the prospect of incarcerating him for the rest of his life.

Alec's curtains had been drawn back, and he lay against his pillows, for once not reading, looking pale and shaky. But he waved cheerfully at us.

'The damned things didn't fit properly, so I've a few days' grace. Must catch up on my reading, I still want to get through *War and Peace* before I die!'

Mr Fenchurch was obviously upset. 'Alec, you musn't talk like that, even in a joke. In a few weeks you'll be able to walk around without even noticing your feet. Really!'

'Oh sure!' Alec said scornfully, but without bitterness. 'I'll be the first bionic footballer in England. I'll be the number one attraction—' He broke off, close to tears, and abruptly turned his back. Mr Fenchurch cleared his throat in embarrassment.

'Well, I must be getting on. Some more coffee?'

'No thanks. It's getting dark again; I can't believe another day has gone. Will it be a quiet night, Sunday?'

'It's in the hands of the Lord,' answered Mr Fenchurch piously, 'but each night I go to sleep knowing it may be my last night. My head grows bigger all the time.' He smiled almost apologetically. 'One night it will burst, of course, and

I dread the mess it will make all over the ward. I've told them about it, but they don't seem to care. I wrote a letter to the Governor of the hospital, but he hasn't replied yet. I just hope he'll be in time.'

I hoped so too; there was something eerie about the very normalcy of Mr Fenchurch. I was relieved when he took my cup and moved his trolley onwards.

The change-over to the night staff was being accomplished in a typical casual manner. Gladys had explained that they came on and went off duty over a period of half an hour, to avoid upsetting the very ill patients who sometimes became panicky if they imagined their nurse was deserting them. I saw Rhoda checking in with the control desk, being acquainted with the latest condition of each patient. I hoped my chart was now optimistic; I had no wish to suffer any more of these ectoplasm stunts, real or imagined.

I felt vaguely cheated; my Big Production had misfired and the final curtain had descended and then risen a few inches off the floor, spoiling the whole effect so that the actors' feet could be seen scurrying ignominiously off the stage. My careful plans now seemed slightly ludicrous, a selfish and cowardly way of getting rid of my problems. At the same time I did not want to become 'a burden to society'. The answer, I suppose, was to do something within my limits and *not* become a burden. Brave words.

Night had closed in and the haze of a million lights softened the skyline. The clicks and hums and muted voices had become a friendly background, and I wished I could stay here, protected from the outside, in a safe cocoon, for the rest of my existence. A curious thought struck me. Perhaps I *was* dead? Could it be that one transferred across to some other continuum, a kind of continuation into another limbo? The idea was appealing. Outside of this ward, was there a world, or was this to be my fate for eternity? I liked the thought; with nurses like Rhoda looking after me, it couldn't be bad.

Inevitably I was attempting to block out reality. Out there

the world hurried on, unaware and uninterested in my little problems, oblivious of the twelve human wrecks who had failed to find peace and who had multiplied their own fears and dilemmas. Alec, if he allowed himself to live, would no doubt come to terms with life and become accustomed to his artificial feet. But what of the young chap in the sports car? His was a living brain imprisoned in a tortured body. He would never see daylight again, probably never walk again, every moment a searing memory of those few tragic seconds when he had driven into the brick wall.

Black, chic Miss Sims came over and wished me good evening. Her slim fingers caressed my wrist as she took my pulse.

'I see they managed to keep you alive until we came back on duty. Had a good day?'

'No. You weren't here. My love over-runneth for my dusky maiden!'

She laughed, low and attractively. 'My! We *are* feeling better! With all that over-running love your pulse is perfectly normal; I'm offended.'

She made a note on the chart. 'I see Dr Marshall has ordered two sleeping-pills. I thought you'd had enough of those!'

It did seem ironic. 'Maybe I'm just queer for pills. But I do find it difficult to sleep with all the noise. Is it going to be a busy night?'

Her face looked sad for a moment. 'Every night is busy here. Sometimes I wonder what the world will be like in fifty years. The more civilized we become, the more the pressure . . .' She became business-like. 'You comfortable? No dizziness or pain anywhere? Your throat getting better?'

I nodded. 'All fine. My throat still hurts, but not as badly. I still have no appetite, though.'

'Not important, you won't need to eat for a day or two yet. Your "drip" is feeding you. First you must get rid of all the poison.' She patted my hand. 'Call if you want anything.'

I lay back and retreated into my own snug world, dreading the time when I would be fit again and have to face the trauma of life once more. Even the thought of standing up and fighting for balance appalled me; if only I could remain in bed forever, tended by these angels; I would promise to be no trouble and could become the ward's mascot; I could even take over the tea trolley and do some useful work. If I hung on to the trolley my balance would be good enough. I liked the idea and determined to talk to Dr Marshall about it. I listened to the Coughing Man barking his throat away and vying with the humming machines and the background music of Mozart's Clarinet Quintet being piped into the ward.

I must have fallen asleep, because consciousness flooded back to a nightmarish sound of screaming. Not exactly screams, a kind of ghoulish wailing of pure agony, as if every sound was being ripped out of the lungs with fiery forceps. I hope never again to hear that agonized, soul-destroying keening, something barely human from the bottomless pit of hell.

It was the burn case who had been brought in the previous night, his face covered with some kind of white foam. He was half sitting up and in the dim light I could see only a pulpy red jelly where his face should have been. Hypnotized by the awful sight, I watched as a nurse tried to inject a hypodermic into a scarred red arm.

The noise had woken most of the patients, and like animals the panic spread. Mr Perry was nearly choking himself trying to get out of bed, his mouth dribbling saliva and his eyes rolling like skittering marbles. The man who was constantly crying out for Jesus to save him was sitting up, his face purple, screaming, 'The time has come! The white-hot finger of God is probing you! Hell has burst its dam and all will perish! Save us, Jesus, save us!' King Kong, despite his restraining sheet, had managed to struggle upright and his pig-eye shone malevolently as his lipless slit yelled obscenities at the ward. Bedlam.

Two interns, hastily summoned by the control desk, entered quickly to assist the nurses. A new patient in a bed opposite had his hands over his ears and was screaming, 'Kill him, kill him, shut him up somehow!' I had the same thought, that dreadful sound of agony was nerve-shattering.

The interns were giving injections while the nurses soothed down the patients. Within a few minutes the noise quietened, the burn victim's cries reduced to a low moan. Throughout all the pandemonium the Coughing Man had lain quietly barking his life away.

The sleeping pills probably helped; it was daylight when I awoke. Within minutes I knew we had a change of cast, that a new production was about to begin.

The burn case, the Coughing Man, and the car-crash victim had all died during the night. A new day had started, but to them it was unimportant now. Their Gehenna was over.

In life one must accept that Death will be the final referee. When that referee is playing several games at the same time one begins to understand how the medical profession can, sometimes, appear callous and detached. To them, day after day, year after year, Death is a constant bedside guest, with no regard to Visiting Hours.

Apparently I had cheated Death twice, and perhaps Pete would have termed it the miracle he wanted to see but in which cynically he never believed. I was not so much concerned or astonished at still being alive, but enormously grateful that I had suffered no brain damage or serious injury. Shortly after nine on that Monday morning, just one week since I had been rushed into the ambulance, the delectable Dr Marshall appeared on her rounds. She was cheerful and bright, but I wondered how many hours sleep she had snatched. I asked her about the consequences if I had lain unconscious much longer.

She regarded me with grim amusement.

'I'd say you probably wouldn't be here now. Your whole system must have been ready to break down. Apart from your heart giving out, your skin would have contused and peeled, and you'd have huge raw sores all over you. As it is, you'll always have a slight scar on your rear, which only your girlfriends will see. Your foot and elbow will probably heal completely, almost without a blemish.'

'And there's no other damage?'

'So far, no. You have a slight loss of feeling on the top of your left foot – when I pricked you there you hardly responded – but that should reactivate in a month or two. As to your innards, tomorrow you'll go down for a complete X-ray, but I'm very hopeful the results will be positive. You've had no pain inside? No sudden stabs?'

'No. Just my chest, it still hurts if I cough.'

She smiled, and the sun lit up the ward. 'That's the beating we gave you in the I.C. Unit. You'll live!'

'How long do I stay here?'

'It depends on you. If you have no more relapses I'd say another ten days or two weeks. Once the poison is completely dissipated you'll improve rapidly.'

I asked her the sixty-four thousand dollar question.

'What about my balance? Is there nothing I can do about that?'

She touched my hand briefly. 'One thing at a time. Let's get you better first of all. Then I'll arrange for you to see Mr Garold, he's our resident E.N.T. specialist. But your problem, your imbalance, is unfortunately purely a physical one. There's no way of putting back the liquid which has been lost.'

'In other words, it's not like a transplant, I can't have an operation to put it right?'

'I'm afraid not,' she said compassionately, 'but I do assure you that in time you'll become more used to it. Human tolerance has a remarkable way of overcoming these problems.'

I tried not to appear irritated. 'In other words, I'm back to the classic advice, "You'll learn to live with it!" '

This time she squeezed my hand. 'Yep. But it's true! In a year or two you'll hardly even notice it. Oh sure, you'll never be a trapeze artist or a mountaineer, and you'll have to give up tennis, but you'll be able to grow old gracefully and I'm damned sure you won't end up in a wheelchair. In other words, although it's up to Mr Garold to confirm this, it's a condition which should *not* deteriorate. It won't get better, but you'll subconsciously adjust to it. Just think of all the people who have massive heart attacks and have to change their whole mode of life. After a while they hardly notice the difference.'

I suppose she was trying to cheer me up, and she succeeded. If what she said was true, life need not be so bad. I began to feel ashamed again of my suicide attempt.

'But for Christ's sake why did that last specialist say I might end up in a wheelchair? That was really the final straw as far as I was concerned!'

She made a wry face. 'Why indeed? Perhaps he thought he ought to prepare you for that possibility. But I'd say it's highly unlikely. Perhaps he didn't realize what you'd been through. Doctors don't always remember their God-like image to the patient.'

She continued on her rounds and I pondered what she had said. Hope is a many-splendoured thing. Perhaps I was fooling myself, but Dr Marshall's words made me feel better.

Dr Payne came briskly into the ward, followed by two interns in crisp white jackets. He was carrying a camera and he made a big point of addressing Mr Perry in a loud voice so that the entire ward could hear. He towered over the little man, holding up the camera above his head.

'Good morning, good morning, my dear Mr Perry! See, I have here the latest invention of modern science, an instrument which can make photographs. This little device is going to cure you of all your ills – marvellous what they think of these days, ain't it?' Theatrically he turned to his assistants. 'Will you be good enough to prepare Mr Perry for his picture?'

To my disappointment the interns pulled the yellow curtains round the bed, cutting off all further sight. The psychiatrist disappeared inside, still talking like a side-show barker. A few minutes later a flashlight went off, and Dr Payne emerged and strode out of the ward. The curtains were pulled back by the interns and I saw Mr Perry lying very quietly on his back, his face a deep puce.

I regarded the rest of the ward with interest. The beds were all occupied, but most of the patients seemed to be sleeping or unconscious. The black preacher on the other side of Alec was sitting up, reading a Bible. Alec himself was writing a letter, and Mr Carstairs, the man with the weak heart who had tried to jump from his apartment, was reading a newspaper. The bed next to him, previously occupied by the Coughing Man, now contained a young man in bright yellow pyjamas who was having a loud argument with Gladys. He had a piercing twang which made me think he was Australian.

'Don't give me that codswallop,' he was saying, 'I know my rights and I want a telephone!'

Gladys placated him, fluffing up his pillows. 'All right, all right! Just give me a minute to connect it up. Who d'you want to call?'

'None of your business, but I'll tell you. I'm calling a newspaper to expose this fuckin' hospital. Now just get me that 'phone, quick!'

I watched Gladys come to the end of the ward and speak to a sister, who nodded. Then she wheeled a portable telephone to the man's bedside and plugged it into the wall. Yellow Pyjamas, without a word of thanks, dialled a number. The sister to whom Gladys had spoken crossed over to the rear of the control board, out of sight of the caller, and lifted a receiver.

'May I help you, sir?'

'Yes, this is Jim Danvers. I want the News Desk. I thought you'd be interested to know I saw a man murdered last night!'

'I'm sorry, sir, you have the wrong number.' The sister put down the receiver and waited. Furiously, Yellow Pyjamas dialled again. Patiently the sister replied, and I listened to the same conversation. After the third attempt, Jim Danvers was becoming frantic with anger. Gladys stopped by my bed.

'He's a card, he is, but we have to humour him.'

I was curious. 'What's he so peeved about? What does he think happened last night?'

She shrugged, her piled-up hair jogging with her breasts.

'He insists he saw one of the interns putting one of the patients out of his misery last night. Wants to report it to the newspapers. Even if he did get through, they'd check back with the hospital first. This way it saves everyone's time.'

'Could there be any truth in it?'

I asked her out of idle curiosity. From my point of view I have always believed in mercy killing, or 'pulling out the plug', and in the case of the car-crash man, it would seem the most merciful act to perform. But I was surprised at Gladys's reaction. Her smile vanished and she busied herself with my chart, then hurried away without answering.

Now I *was* curious. What *had* Jim Danvers seen? Or was it pure imagination, a patient being given an injection and then dying shortly afterwards? I turned to my source of information, Alec.

'That chap must have come in last night. He seems fairly *compos mentis*, what's wrong with him?'

Alec laid down his pen. 'Funny you should ask. He's supposed to have taken an overdose, but he's recovered awfully quickly. Personally, I suspect he's a newspaperman trying to get an inside story.'

Our attention was diverted by Dr Payne, who came into the ward and stood inside the swing doors, brandishing a large photograph.

'Ladies and Gentlemen,' he announced, waiting until conversation had died, 'I am going to show Mr Perry his latest photograph. I would like everyone to listen.'

He crossed to Mr Perry and held the picture in front of his eyes. 'Look well, Mr Perry, here is a photograph of yourself being hung up and strangled. Notice the rubber cable round your scrawny neck, and you can just see the hands of my friend Joe hauling the cable up above your head. See how your eyes are bulging, and how the wire is cutting into your Adam's apple. Another few seconds and you would have been dead.'

The ward was very quiet, the hum of machines providing a sinister background.

Dr Payne surveyed the ward slowly.

'Mr Perry from now onwards has given up swearing, and he no longer wants to destroy property. He will eat his food like any other human being, and he will become one of the friendliest men alive. So I want all of you who can walk and talk to converse with Mr Perry whenever you can.'

He paused and looked at Mr Perry. 'But, if he forgets his manners for one moment . . . then a nurse will show him this photograph and immediately call me so that we can hang him up again.'

There was a long pause. 'Now, Mr Perry, what were you going to say to me?'

There was another silence. Mr Perry wet his lips and seemed to look around for help. I felt sorry for the little man, but no doubt the psychiatrist knew what he was doing. Eventually he closed his eyes and whispered: 'Good morning, Doctor.'

There was a tangible sigh through the ward, a milestone had been passed. A nurse clapped her hands loudly, everyone who had been able to listen started to talk again. Dr Payne slapped him on the shoulder and held up his hand for silence.

'Good fellow! So now you're an ordinary patient, and this strait-jacket's coming off and you can use your hands and feed yourself. Just make sure you say "please" and "thank you" to the nurses!'

Mr Perry looked dumbfounded. Doctor Payne leaned close to him and probably only I heard what he whispered: 'Just remember! Make one mistake again and I swear I'll hang you up until you wish you *were* dead!' He turned and stalked out of the ward, a nice dramatic exit.

A sister and two nurses came across to the old man, chattering warmly while they released him, plumping up his pillows. He was handed a glass of orange juice, which quaveringly he took in his free hands and drank, still stunned. I turned to Alec. He looked at me smugly.

'I knew old Payne would find a cure. I bet the old fellow gets out before we do!'

I saw Jim Danvers, the Australian nuisance, coming across to our side of the ward. He was holding a clip-board and pen. He had sharp features, with eyes too close together, which my grandmother always said was a sign to distrust. He stopped at the foot of my bed.

'You're okay, aren't you? Were you awake last night?'

I should have told him to push off, but I had a curious defenceless sensation, as if I was a new boy at school and he was the local bully. I answered him cautiously.

'Some of the time. Why?'

'Did you see what happened about three this morning? They clobbered that guy in the plaster. I'm getting up a petition and I want you to sign it.'

Despite my repugnance, I was interested to know what he had seen. 'I didn't see anything. What was it you saw?'

'All the nurses suddenly left the ward, except for the one on Control, and she kept her back to the bed. There was a sort of whistle, then a guy in a white jacket came through from over there—' he indicated a door in the corner of the ward which Alec had told me led to the staff rest-room. 'He went straight over to the plaster patient, bent over him for about half a minute, then scarpered out. The whistle sounded again, and all the nurses came back in. One of them covered over the patient and in two ticks they came and hauled him away. It was real spooky, all silent; they knew he was dead.'

'Well, I'm sorry, but I can't sign anything. I was asleep at that time.'

He muttered something angrily, but moved over to Alec's bed. I felt ice cold and lay back staring at the overhead gantries of spotlights and cameras.

I had *not* been asleep at that time. And I very distinctly remembered hearing the two whistles, and noticing there were no nurses around.

Retribution came to Jim Danvers very swiftly and with a Kafkaesque awesomeness. He was sitting up in his bed, busy writing on his clipboard, when the swing doors opened and four distinguished-looking men strode in. One of them had a brief word with a sister, who nodded towards the Australian's bed. Jim looked up in surprise as the four men surrounded him, making no attempt to lower their voices. A portly one in his sixties with flowing white hair appeared to be the spokesman.

'Mr Danvers, we represent the Board of Governors of this hospital. It has come to our notice that you have attempted to convey a slanderous message to one of the daily newspapers.'

Danvers did not seem too cowed by this accusation.

'Dam' right I did, mate! You don't expect to see patients being bumped off in the middle of the night.' He grinned slyly at them. 'Got my proof, too!'

Whitehair harrumphed pompously. 'Rubbish! What you think you saw was imagination. You were under drugs and hallucinating.'

'Balls. I know exactly what I saw, and the newspaper will love this story.'

One of the other men stepped forward.

'Are you a reporter?'

Danvers placed his forefinger against his nose in a gesture of secrecy. 'Shan't tell!'

'In that case,' announced Whitehair, 'I must ask you to get dressed and be discharged from this hospital. We strongly suspect that your symptoms were faked, and you are perfectly fit to leave. But I warn you, if you attempt to foist your ridiculous story on the media, in any way whatsoever, you will receive an immediate summons for libel from our legal advisers. Good day, sir!'

Solemnly they trooped out, leaving an unrepentant Danvers. I wondered why it had necessitated four of them to deliver their warning. Danvers slid out of bed and crossed to Alec, who had also been watching this drama.

'Alec, mate, you keep an eye on things. This isn't the first incident we've heard about, but I had to see for myself. You notice that happen again, keep a note of the date and the exact time and you contact me as soon as you get out. Ring me at this number.' He handed a card to Alec, who non-committally put it on his bedside table. Danvers returned to his bed, where a nurse had brought in his street clothes. There was little conversation in the ward as he dressed. I think most of us felt we had been betrayed in some way, as if a stranger had infiltrated our tight little world; certainly no one seemed shocked or in sympathy with his alleged scandal. Alec put it simply when he whispered across to me.

'Silly twerp, what's he trying to stir up? If it *is* true, good luck to the hospital! I'm sure those poor bastards would agree as well; *they* didn't want to live in agony.'

I couldn't help but agree with him. I watched as Jim Danvers picked up a small suitcase and made for the door. He gave a mock salute to the ward, which nobody returned. A nurse accompanied him down to the entrance, presumably to make sure he finally left the building. The piped music had changed to a spirited Debussy Prelude – *Fireworks*, I think it was – and conversation returned to normal while the ward went about its business of living and dying. I turned back to Alec.

'You think it's true, and that it often happens? That they put some patients out of their agony?'

He stared at me, his young-old face unusually serious. 'Not often, because normally nature takes its course and the patient will die within hours anyway. But just occasionally there's a freak case where the body or mind is almost destroyed, impossible to mend, but where the guy may continue legally to live, maybe for months or even years, but totally incapable of moving. I think that's when the doctors show some mercy.'

I shuddered inwardly, but more for the doctor who had to make that choice. I remembered reading a book by a German author about the hospital near Stuttgart where the casualties of World War II were looked after, the really grim ones. There was a special room where the patients, mainly Air Force, were kept if they had lost their arms and legs. Instead of beds, they were encased in special sacks and hung from rails. Without any limbs the body is incapable of moving, but to be upright was healthier for the torso than lying flat. Some of these poor remains of human beings had been there for years. Many of them were blind and in constant pain, scarred and burned by the crash which had amputated their limbs, but this sacred necessity to save human lives had deprived them of merciful oblivion.

For years 'mercy killing' has been argued back and forth, those against it quoting the moral, religious and legal aspects. But the fact remains that in almost one hundred per cent of cases, if the victim could be consulted, he would opt out. Is it kind or merciful to keep a soul trapped in a useless body? Even less so if the mind is dead; with hospitals overcrowded and ill people waiting desperately for beds, why use up valuable doctor-time, constant attendance by nurses, rare drugs and expensive machinery, and above all, space which could otherwise be valuably used, to keep alive a hulk?

The moralists will always win, until a more sane and rational society exists. But in my own small world, I was sure that the car-crash youth would have wanted it this way.

Gladys appeared at my bedside carrying a small portable electric razor.

'You look a bit scruffy! D'you want to grow a beard or would you like to shave?'

'Bless you, I'd like to shave. This fungus itches and I've always hated beards.'

The razor was not over-sharp, and I had accumulated quite a stiff bristle. Finally, however, I had a smooth face again and felt better for it. I was looking forward to when I could have a shower. The sponge baths each morning were messy and inadequate.

The day passed slowly. Mr Perry seemed to be fighting some battle of his own. He lay passively for most of the time, but occasionally he would mumble to himself and then try to get out of bed, the restraining cord pulling him back. But I noticed that he made no attempt to tear any papers, although Gladys had put some periodicals beside him. It seemed like a good sign. At lunch-time they gave him a bowl of soup, which he ate slowly, using his own hands. It looked as if Dr Payne's unorthodox cure might succeed.

King Kong, who I imagined was being kept heavily sedated, roused himself towards the end of the afternoon and again started screaming oaths at everyone. His strength was incredible, for at a certain moment he managed to free his left hand and started tearing at the restraining sheet. Within seconds nurses had dealt with him, one giving an injection while another pressed him back on to the pillow and talked soothingly to him. My admiration for these young girls was enormous.

Twice each day I was turned on my stomach and had the dressing changed on my rear end. Although I could not see it myself, it was apparently a fiery red welt, surrounded by a purple sunset, which Gladys and the other nurses exclaimed at with sadistic delight. My foot and elbow sores were much smaller, but more painful; I had to be careful not to lean on my right elbow otherwise an excruciating flash of pain would shoot up my arm. Curiously, I almost welcomed it, as it reminded me how lucky I had been compared to some of the others in the ward.

The black preacher, who had tried to cut his throat, was allowed up and he slowly circled the room in a tattered old dressing-gown. He held his head stiffly, his neck encased in bandages. He stopped by my bed and waved a black hand.

'Good evening, friend. May I talk to you?'

'Of course. Get yourself a chair if you like.'

'No, I've rested enough.' He smiled, a beautiful smile which lit up his rather ugly face. He appeared so gentle I found it hard to believe he had seriously tried to slit his own throat. He continued, 'It's time I returned to my duties.'

'Are you well enough to leave yet?'

'As well as I'll ever be. At least the pain has subsided for now. I think God was trying to tell me something.'

I always get embarrassed when people are in touch with God. Pete's philosophy I could understand, but I still found it difficult to believe that God had time to talk to any one human being. He would be very busy answering all those hundreds of millions of prayers. But the preacher seemed quietly confident that he had found his answers. He must have sensed my thoughts.

'It's good that I talk to someone, if you'll bear with me. Probably we'll never meet again, but for a brief moment our lives have touched, even in these unhappy circumstances. I live in the north of England, and I came to London to do away with myself in private, so as not to distress my flock. Unfortunately, my plans miscarried.'

Now I *was* curious. 'Can I ask why? You must have had a very strong reason.' A less likely would-be suicide was difficult to imagine.

Again the beautiful smile. 'Cowardice was my reason. I have terminal cancer of the bowels, and the pain had become overwhelming. Even the drugs were useless. There seemed no point spending the last month or two in agony; the medication and drugs were so strong I could not carry on with my work. I decided that God would understand if I arrived a little early.'

'But are you sure? Is it really terminal? These days they can do a helluva lot to check it.'

'It's much too far advanced, I'm afraid. My own fault, I ignored all the warnings, trying to deceive myself it was the recurrence of an ulcer which I had earlier in my life. The hospital doctors in my home town said it could only be a matter of weeks now. I wouldn't mind, if only the pain was not so severe. But now I can face it; perhaps I'm being tested in some way.'

I didn't have the heart to disillusion him. If God was so damned merciful, why put this poor bastard through a course of sheer agony? But, like all religion, a man who trusts can never be betrayed, he can only be mistaken.

There was perspiration on his brow, and I realized that even while he stood talking he was very evidently in pain.

'Will you go back to your own hospital?'

'Only as an out-patient to obtain the drugs. My faith is

now so strong I can conquer the pain, and at least carry on with my work for a little longer. Thank you for listening to me.' He gave a stiff bow and slowly walked back to his bed, his hands clenched and his head held rigid. I hoped he would have enough faith to win his battle.

Alec had listened to the conversation and he shook his head sorrowfully. 'There goes a brave man! I wouldn't envy facing my congregation with a bloody great scar across my throat. He'd be better off dying in hospital!'

'Atonement, Alec. He's obviously got a huge guilt complex, perhaps that's how he'll face his agony.'

The day shift was gradually departing, and I saw Rhoda emerge from the nurses' rest-room, looking crisp and gorgeous as usual. I suppose in my weakened state almost any nurse would have looked glamorous, but I was willing to bet that in the street, out of uniform, she would still be a knockout. I was incredibly glad when she came across to my bed.

'Hi, there! You've got some colour back! Feeling better?' She studied my chart and I wished I could say something which would make me a person instead of just another patient.

'Much better, thanks. What do you do in your spare time?'

She laughed her tinkling laugh. 'What spare time? I sleep! Blessed, wonderful sleep, which I never get enough of!'

'Will you come to the theatre with me, and dinner afterwards, when I leave here?'

'My, that's the best offer I've had all day. Let's wait till you get out. Then you'll have all your girlfriends to take care of.'

But at least she hadn't destroyed my hopes by saying she had a jealous boyfriend or a husband around. It was a ridiculous fantasy of mine, but at least I could cherish it a little longer. I caught a faint whiff of perfume – Arpège? – as she bent over to rearrange my pillows.

'You're outrageously beautiful,' I told her, 'no wonder my pulse and temperature are all to hell!'

Now she blushed. 'Will you shut up and behave like a normal patient? It's bad enough coping with the ill ones without having a sex maniac like you. Where's your wife, anyway?'

I tried to look sad and unwanted. 'Probably with a friend of mine. I don't suppose she knows I'm here.'

It had the desired effect. Rhoda took my hand and pressed it warmly. 'I'm sorry! I shouldn't have said that. It's just such a relief to talk to someone who's facing up to reality in here.'

I didn't disillusion her. Reality was something in the future; meanwhile I wanted only to be part of this strange world which ended in the swing doors leading to the corridor to Outside. I wanted to remain forever, to be accepted into the Graveyard Club, to be part of the warm twenty-four-hour cocoon.

There seemed to be no official visiting hours in the ward and, in fact, there were few visitors. Perhaps relatives were discouraged by the authorities until a patient was well on the way to recovery. I had noticed an attractive girl who had twice visited Alec, but each time she had drawn the curtains round the bed for privacy, and Alec himself had offered no information about her.

So it was with surprise, as dusk was creeping in the windows, that I saw Pete entering the ward. He was in jeans and sloppy sweater. He crossed over to the nurse on control duty and spoke briefly to her. She nodded and indicated my bed. He came over, a large grin on his face.

'Man, you've lost weight! You look a lot better!'

'Thanks a bunch, Pete, but it's a tough way to go on a diet!'

He sat on the edge of the bed. 'Can I smoke in here?'

'Yes, there are no rules and regulations, thank God. We're a very friendly club. Did you bring a bottle of cognac with you?'

He laughed, his wise young eyes watching me. He took out a packet and lit a cigarette, being careful to blow the smoke away from me. 'You sure gave us all a surprise! Was your balance really that bad?'

Somehow I didn't mind discussing it with Pete; and the

inevitable time would come when I'd have to face my friends and colleagues again. 'Perhaps not, in retrospect. It just seemed a good idea at the time. I didn't want to grow old in a wheelchair.'

He shook his head wonderingly. 'Man! You're a card! You have everything to live for, but you let a little thing like vertigo get you down. Why didn't you discuss it with someone?'

'Because, chum, suicide isn't something you announce to the world in advance. Not if you're serious about it, and I *was*.'

'And are you still?'

I shrugged, giving a wince of pain as the tube in my chest pulled at the plaster. 'Not to worry! I've seen enough in here to realize it's not the right answer. I'm just thankful I didn't wake up a vegetable. Perhaps that was the miracle we talked about!'

'It's grim, is it?' He looked around the ward curiously. At the moment it was fairly quiet, and it was difficult to see the shattered bodies and minds which occupied some of the beds. It could have been an ordinary ward in any hospital. 'I gather all these cases are would-be suicides?'

'Yes, incredibly so. And as fast as they die more are brought in. It makes you think that modern society is not all it's cracked up to be. I've had time to do a lot of thinking. There must be an awful amount of unhappiness if this happens every day all over the country!' I didn't mean to pontificate, but Pete seemed to know what I was trying to say.

'You're right, it's a sad reflection on a so-called civilized world. I read recently that in America the highest proportion of suicides was amongst dentists! How come?'

'Nobody loves a dentist!' I joked, 'Perhaps they're more sensitive than we think. Tell me, have you seen Josh? What's happening in the office?'

'They're fine, wanting you back as soon as possible. I'm not supposed to discuss any business with you, I only got in here because I said I was your local Godsman. I had to show my papers and even then they hardly believed it. I suppose I should have got tarted up in my white collar!'

It hurt to laugh, but I could imagine Pete in his old clothes trying to get past Reception. He crossed to Alec's table and carefully mashed out his cigarette in an ashtray. He looked at his watch as he returned. 'I must go, they only gave me ten minutes. Is there anything I can get you? D'you want to see anyone?'

'Not yet, thanks. Maybe in a day or two. I feel fine, but I get this awful desire to blub at any emotional contact. Damned silly.'

He grinned. 'Probably good for you, getting rid of all your guilt complexes. There's some good-looking broads around here, I can see you're being well looked after!'

Miss Sims came up to my bed and regarded Pete with a slightly disdainful air.

'I think your time is up, Reverend, or were you planning to bed down with us for the night?' Her impish smile softened her tone. Pete clasped his hands together in mock horror.

'If only I could, Sister, if only I could. But with a figure like yours it would be unfair to face such temptation!'

'On your way, you awful man! I think God must be slipping up somewhere.'

When Pete had left she came back to my bedside.

'He's a wonderful man, your friend. You know he's been haunting this hospital all week, waiting to see you? He even gave a special service in the Chapel downstairs to offer up prayers for you and the others in this ward.'

Of course I began to cry.

It was nearly midday the next morning before Fred arrived to take me to the X-ray department. Apparently it was one of the busiest in the hospital, and unless it was an emergency, patients had to be booked in and wait their turn to be examined and photographed.

It had been a quieter night, and I slept well. The noise of the oscilloscope machines, as I learnt they were called, no longer bothered me, and I took a proprietary interest in watching the fluorescent blips racing across the screens.

Tessa, the black nurse with the north-country accent, had changed my dressings, sponged my back, and then removed the intravenous drip line from my chest. The sharp needle at the end, attached to a blood vessel, came out surprisingly painlessly, and she slapped a small piece of plaster over the cut. I had become so used to moving carefully, so as not to disturb it, that I felt as if I had been released from some kind of bondage. The drip in my arm had been removed the previous day.

'You'll start getting hungry by tomorrow,' she informed me, 'but begin with soup only, and lots of tea with plenty of sugar.'

Fred arrived with a wheelchair. I was helped out of bed, finding my legs like rubber and experiencing the now familiar balance problem as I stood up. I pulled on a heavy dressing-gown which Gladys brought, and thankfully subsided on to the chair.

It was a peculiar sensation to leave the ward. I felt as if I had been there for many weeks, and I was mentally naked and afraid as we sped down the long corridor. I expected everyone we met to glare at me and point a finger of scorn, but no one seemed interested. We descended to the basement in one of the large elevators, Fred keeping up a running commentary.

'See that button there, mate? That's fer 'mergencies, cuts aht orl the other calls, so's yer don't stop at every floor. These lifts travel a fousand miles a year, makes yer think. Some of them 'ave done fifty fousand miles, better than a bleedin' car. Got stuck in one once, a patient on the way to an op, I didn't arf get 'ell from the O.R. Super fer being late. No bleedin' justice sometimes. Then ther' wuz the time ...'

My powers of concentration were still off-key. The noise of hurrying people and rapid conversation beat on me as nurses, patients, doctors and visitors entered and departed at each floor, the systole and diastole and organized chaos of a busy hospital where rigid schedules ruled and delay was a dedicated enemy.

Eventually I was wheeled into a large space in the basement, off which ran several corridors, each one marked with a signpost. We took the passage marked X-RAY DEPARTMENT, by-passing another corridor which bore the grim legend TERMINAL RECEPTIVE AREA. Fred found it amusing.

'Call a spade a spade, says I. All it means is that it's the mortuary. Bleedin' cold in there, gives me the creeps.'

It gave me the creeps too. I wondered how many shrouded bodies found their way down here each day. It didn't help when we passed another corridor leading to PATHOLOGIST SECTION.

Suddenly we were in a wide and brightly lit reception room. About a dozen patients in wheelchairs were lined up like a Grand Prix starting grid. Nurses were circulating, making notes, and intermittently a loudspeaker would crackle into life summoning the next patient. Fred wheeled me into line, said a cheery good-bye, and picked up a wheelchair whose occupant was waiting to return to a ward.

After fifteen minutes another attendant swooped on me and wheeled me off down a long passage. In the X-ray room I was lifted on to a cold and extremely hard table and machines with giant eyes glared down at me. By then I was feeling tired and sleepy and wished I was safely back in bed.

It took about twenty minutes, efficient nurses and lab attendants turning me into strange positions, ordering me to keep still, telling me not to breathe, then I found myself out in the corridor behind a long line of wheelchairs. The nurse tucked a blanket round me. 'Wait here for a few minutes until we get the all-clear from the labs that your pictures were satisfactory. Then you'll be taken back to your ward.'

In a few minutes I was back in The Graveyard. Alec gave me a thumbs-up sign and Bossy Boots helped me into bed. I felt as if I had run ten miles.

Little old Mr Perry seemed to be rehabilitating himself. The nurses were making a big fuss over him, and he ate his lunch placidly, although Gladys hovered near him. He had a newspaper beside him, which I was glad to see was in one piece. Certainly it looked as if Dr Payne's drastic cure had been highly effective.

About four in the afternoon the Floor Matron came bustling in and approached Mr Perry.

'My dear man, you realize today is your birthday! We're having a little celebration and guess who's come to celebrate with you!' She paused dramatically, eyeing him carefully. 'Your daughter wants to give you her best wishes!'

Mr Perry recoiled as if he had been struck, seeming to shrink down in the bed. His mouth moved spasmodically.

'Teresa? Teresa is here?' he whispered. 'What's she doing here? I can't see her!'

'Of course you can,' boomed Matron, 'she's come down from Manchester just for the occasion.' She crossed to the swing doors and beckoned outside. A timid and rather large woman of middle age entered. Mr Perry tried to hide under the bedclothes, his gaunt eyes peering over the top of the sheet. The woman approached uncertainly, smiling.

'Dad! Dad, it's wonderful to see you! You're looking fine. Happy Birthday!'

Then the doors opened again and Bossy Boots came in holding a cake with lighted candles. All the nurses started to sing 'Happy Birthday to You', and Mr Fenchurch followed them in with the tea trolley. Chairs were pulled up and several of the nurses sat down around the bed.

Mr Perry emerged from the sheet, looking like a scared mouse who knows it's all a cruel joke and the sword of Damocles will descend at any moment. His daughter leaned forward and kissed him.

'Go on, Pops, blow them out! You're coming back to live with us!'

There was a hushed silence as the ward watched the old man. It seemed as if we were all willing him to respond. His rheumy eyes glanced at the cake, at his daughter, at the Matron. Then he pursed his mouth and weakly started blowing out the candles. His daughter leant forward to help him.

There was a round of clapping and again Mr Perry shrank back as if he was about to be hit. Prudently the Matron did not offer him a knife, but took the cake to a side table to cut it. She handed the first piece to him, and still disbelieving, he bit into it. Suddenly he started to weep. The nurses started chatting and laughing, tactfully ignoring the little man as his daughter ran her hand through his sparse hair.

An hour later I was lying back, half asleep and wondering if I could take up my career again or whether I would be treated as a dangerous pariah. I had never thought much about suicides before, or how the unsuccessful ones returned to society. If anything, I knew I would have tried to avoid a would-be suicide, just as one tries to avoid a cripple or, presumably, a leper. One feels pity for them, but life is complicated enough without becoming involved further. It's a coward's way out, but lying in hospital it was time to assess one's values and face a few facts of life.

Once I had tried to help at a charity show for spastic children. I had obtained the services of several famous people, who gladly gave their time, free, to help such a good cause. I had been there myself to make sure everything went smoothly, but I did not reckon on the profound effect it had on me, to see these half-beings, some of them mongoloid, trying to live a hopeless life. My admiration for the people who looked after them, year after year, was enormous, but it upset me so much I took the easy way out and left early. I had nightmares for weeks afterwards.

The Floor Matron returned to the ward and made a brief round. She stopped by my bed and indicated Mr Perry, who was now sleeping peacefully.

'It was a big day for him. He'll go back to live with his daughter and son-in-law. I don't envy them.'

'But surely he's cured? He was like a lamb today.'

She sighed, a sad sigh born of grim experience.

'Yes, because kindness can work wonders. His daughter had turned him out of the house because he was so rude and belligerent. He'll go back now and everything will be fine for a few days or a few weeks. But he has a long record of petty violence, and the day will come when an argument starts. Either with his family or a stranger. After all, you can't go around with a placard saying: "I'm ill, please be kind to me." '

'You think he's actually insane?'

'No. But we know very little about insanity or the human brain. I think he's mentally unstable, and just one destructive word will upset him. I hope I'm wrong.'

I began to realize how difficult it must be to assess a cure. As she had indicated, he might be perfectly normal for a few weeks, and then the brain would be triggered off by some slight remark which a 'normal' person would probably ignore. What was normality? Was a man who liked big breasts any different to a man who preferred long legs? Was a homosexual any better or worse than a man who liked young girls? Was someone who beat up his own wife more 'normal' than one who committed adultery with his neighbour's wife? Where *was* the norm? Mr Perry's case was slightly different, but who was to know why and when his brain would veer from its normal tolerance, converting him from a kindly old man into a potentially dangerous human being.

That evening I experimented with my first 'meal'. When dinner was served, the ward Sister in charge, a stern-looking woman of about thirty-five, came across and checked my charts. She was tall and thin, with little charm, but occasionally she had flashes of humour. I felt she was extremely shy and reserved but, of course, highly efficient in her job. Tonight she seemed to be more relaxed. She regarded me thoughtfully.

'Lazybones, I see. I think it's time you had something to eat and tried getting up. Tomorrow I want you walking round the ward! We'll start with some of our famous soup.'

She crossed to a trolley and brought back a bowl of thick soup and a spoon. Since my I.V. tube had been removed, I was beginning to feel pangs of hunger. I tasted it gently. It was hot and thick and creamy, with no flavour at all. But it felt good.

'Could I have some salt? It has no taste!'

She sighed. 'Complaints, complaints! It's very good for you and you won't get any salt, yet.' She leant forward in a confidential manner. 'It does taste pretty foul, but just think of it as good medicine. Tomorrow I'll see you get some special food!'

I liked the feeling of eating again, each mouthful seeming to slide down, easing the pain in my throat. It must have been the first food I had taken in over ten days. I had almost finished the bowl when King Kong came to life suddenly.

A nurse had been feeding him when he reared up and knocked the dish out of her hand. His hands were free and he grasped her round the neck. Once again I cringed at that awful face, the solitary eye blinking rapidly and the tiny mouth in the hairless face pouting like a baby. Invalid or not, he almost lifted the nurse off the floor by her neck.

There was a shocked silence round the room. The control nurse whispered into her microphone and I knew expert help would be there within seconds. King Kong seemed to sense this.

'Don't let anyone come near me, I'll kill her before you can do anything!' I saw with horror that the nurse was Gladys, her face now purple as she tried to breathe, lying half across the bed with King Kong's huge hands wrapped tightly round her throat. The ward Sister moved up slowly, talking gently; two interns came quietly into the room, hypodermics ready. A doctor who had been visiting a patient slipped out of his white coat in order to be unrecognizable as a medic.

'Mr Siberius,' said the ward Sister softly, 'what is it you want? Let go of that nurse, she was only trying to help you.'

'Fuck off and leave me alone!' The words came from King Kong with hissing venom. 'Just leave me alone! I want to die, why do you bastards have to interfere? Can't you realize that I don't want to be saved? I *want* to die. Let me die, why are you torturing me like this?'

Gladys had commenced coughing, a strangled, choking coughing which echoed round the ward. King Kong's hands tightened round her htroat. I watched, paralysed at the awful scene, the ward now deathly quiet except for an incongruous Strauss waltz providing a gay and unemotional background.

'We're not torturing you. Why do you want to die? Life is a very precious thing!'

The single eye turned malevolently on the ward Sister. 'Why? You ask why? Just look at me! You would like to go around looking like me? Have people shrink away? I'm eighteen years old, seven feet tall, one eye, hideous, I have no cock and can't even fuck a blind woman. You make me shit!'

The swing doors burst open and Dr Payne strode through, fast and energetic, straight up to the bed. It was obviously a rehearsed ploy. He thrust the ward Sister aside and screamed at King Kong.

'Put that girl down at once, you stupid cunt. She's Government property and they'll put you in jail for twenty years, and see how you like *that*! You can *see*, can't you? What about that fellow in the next bed, he *can't* see! And in *that* bed, he'll never walk again! Stop being so fucking sorry for yourself!'

The sheer attack of the psychiatrist unnerved the big man. He released his grip on Gladys and the interns moved in. Within seconds King Kong had been injected and the crisis was over. Gladys was helped into the nurses' rest-room and the ward returned to normal. Alec turned to me.

'Quite good entertainment today. Our Dr Payne is quite a professional; it's a pity Hughie Green's show is finished, King Kong would have been a riot on it.'

I was still mentally shaking from the sheer suddenness of the outburst. 'But what will they do with him? He's violent, isn't he? Will they report this to the police?'

'Unlikely. It happens often. You'd be surprised how well they're equipped to deal with these wild cases. They even have a kind of gun shooting a doped dart in case someone tries to hold a nurse as a hostage. Very effective!'

Alec was really unbelievable. He seemed to know everything and accept all these tragedies of life as a passing show, to be savoured and criticized like a theatrical première. Again I wondered whether he intended to rehabilitate himself or whether he would go out in a burst of glory the moment he was released from the hospital.

'Alec,' I said softly, 'don't you have any pity or sympathy for these people?'

He regarded me as if I was slightly retarded. 'Whatever for? Everyone in this ward is here because of his own stupidity; he's created his own environment and lives with his own failure. Why should we be pitied? For not being dead? Or because we failed and we're still alive? Are *you* glad that you botched it up and are still alive?'

It was a loaded question which I had not yet truly faced.

Assuming I had no further relapses or complications I would walk out of the hospital within two weeks, to start life again. How would my friends react? Would I just walk back into the office one day and say: 'Hi! fellows, I've been away for a few weeks, how's everything?' Continue with the production of *Misty Horizon*, trying to ignore my imbalance, every day afraid of actually falling over, fighting the exhaustion that came from hours of concentrating on walking in a straight line?

The thought depressed me and I had no answer to Alec's question. How splendid it would be just to fade out and have no more problems. Instinctively I glanced up at the battens of lights to see if 'he' was there, laughing at me, waiting like Mr Jordan to lead me onwards. Had I really heard that voice, or was I hallucinating? Gladys had told me I had 'died' for nearly a minute, meaning my heart had actually stopped beating.

Then I realized I was being impractical and self-pitying. I knew I would never try suicide again, if only through pure fear of failing and waking up with some terrible added affliction. This time I had been let off with a warning.

It was time to reassess my own values; I could see, hear, and speak. I could walk with two legs, if somewhat groggily. I had two hands and a brain. I could smell flowers and taste delicious food. What the hell was I complaining about?

I turned back to the cynical Alec.

'Yes, Alec, I'm glad I botched it up, and I'm delighted that I'm still alive!'

But the day ended depressingly. It had grown dark and Miss Sims and a nurse were making their nightly 'pill' round when there was a curious coughing sound from the opposite side of the ward. Idly I heard a warning buzzer sounding, and two nurses rushed over to Mr Fenchurch's bed. The yellow curtains were hastily pulled round, and a moment later a doctor hurried in.

They took Mr Fenchurch away fifteen minutes later. He had killed himself by plunging a fork through his throat.

It seemed to be a quiet night, or else I slept better than usual. The previous day I had not caught up on the daily gossip, and had no idea whether we had had 'a change of cast' again. I saw that Mr Fenchurch's bed was now occupied by an ominously still figure, and wondered again at the frailty of human nature.

I had never encountered this side of life before. Death, to me, had always been old age, or, in the case of the war, a necessary evil which one grew to accept. I had seen my beloved grandmother die at the age of ninety-two, and been thankful for it, because in one year she changed from being a lovable martinet into a sad and stupid old woman. My father had died suddenly through intestinal cancer, and my mother, at the age of seventy-five, fell and broke her hip. She had become bedridden and I swear she decided to die; in the few months that she, a brilliant tennis and golf player, was confined to her bed, she became obsessively morose and the doctors said afterwards she just gave up any desire to live.

One accepted these happenings, cruel or sad as they were, because age wearies all of us eventually, and only Death can win the final game. But The Graveyard, this ward of half-returns, was a living blot of conscience on our society; and I presumed that every large hospital throughout the country had such a ward, perpetually filled with humans who found their life valueless.

I was alive, still in this world. I hung on to this thought, this belief that I had survived and was here for a purpose. I kept thinking of God, although I was a hopeless agnostic and I wanted to find some proof that I had been saved for some valid reason. Just some sign, some indication that I should have died by my own hand, but it was not to be; some higher power had kept me alive, against all medical rationality, for a Purpose. God in his button-backed armchair had singled me out, hadn't He?

The various doctors had made their rounds and it was nearing lunch-time. Today I was to have soup and a boiled egg, and the expectation was making me salivate.

Quite unexpectedly the swing doors opened and I gawped as my mother-in-law entered. She was carrying a smart shopping bag and, as usual, looked as if she had been having tea at Buck House. I had always liked her, although she seemed to live in a world of her own. Perhaps she was smarter than most people. She saw me at once and walked across, ignoring the rest of the ward as if I was the only occupant.

'My dear boy, you look dreadful! Whatever are they feeding you?' I was glad to see she was wearing her glasses, which she badly needed, but which her pride refused to accept. She took them off and laid them on my bedside table.

'Gloria told me you were in hospital to have some tests for your balance. Why aren't you in a private ward? I mean, all these people around you!'

Obviously my wife had not told her the real reason. I blessed her for that, because Mama would never have understood it. Amongst her horsey crowd one did *not* commit suicide.

'I like it here,' I said warmly, 'it's much more fun than being on one's own.'

She sat on the edge of the bed. 'I mustn't stay long. I'm on my way to a committee meeting, but I thought I'd drop in and bring you a few goodies.' She rummaged in the Fortnum and Mason's carrier bag. 'Here's a little caviar and an avocado, and some calves'-foot jelly. Now, I've also been to the chemist to get you some of those new pills they're advertising on television, full of vitamins. And some of those heartburn pills, Gloria said you suffered from heartburn—' She broke off and looked thoughtful, patting her grey hair in exasperation. 'Or was it Ralph told me, maybe it was his wife.' Ralph was her son. 'Oh dear, well, they'll do you good anyway.'

'Thank you, Mama, you're too kind. I appreciate it very much.'

She brought out a small white bottle.

'I know what it's like in hospital. Now in case you're not going regularly, I brought you some Carters Little Liver Pills. I always swear by them. You remember what my grandfather used to say: "Not rudely swift, nor insolently slow!"'

She set up the bottles on my table, a row of soldiers to make me well again. 'We have a crisis at home, poor Gertrude is pregnant.' I remembered it was the brown spaniel. 'I can't understand it, there are no other spaniels in the district, and Gertrude would never mix with any other dogs.'

'How is Gloria?' I asked. 'You know that we've parted?'

She took out a wisp of a handkerchief and blew her nose. 'You silly boy, everyone has little quarrels sometimes! She's coming round to see you. Just kiss and make up!'

As Gloria was living with another man I very much doubted this would be the case, but there was no point in upsetting her eternally optimistic mother, who saw the entire world through a pink glow of goodness, and refused to countenance any evil or unpleasantness. Her husband, a retired professor and a mild man who pottered through his books and his garden, had recently pressed the accelerator of his car by mistake and driven through their greenhouse. Sitting dazed amongst the wreckage, he had listened while his wife scolded him for destroying some of her precious gardenias.

'It's sweet of you to drop in, Mama, and I appreciate the goodies. Did Gloria say when she was coming?'

'No, I just talked to her on the telephone, you know how busy she is these days. What did they say about your balance? You don't think it's due to too much drink? I lose my balance after two sherries. Perhaps you should change to a good brandy, my father had the same trouble with whisky, but when he changed to brandy he could drink all night; so tiresome, not having a good balance. Mind you, I hate heights, I always get sick and have a vertigo problem when I go up the Eiffel Tower. How does it affect you?'

'I've never been up the Eiffel Tower, and really don't want to. I'm allergic to elevators. Besides, it sways at the top and I'd get sea-sick.'

She shrieked with laughter. I cringed down in the bed and hoped she would leave for her committee meeting. Luckily she did.

'Well, I must away. Eat well and get better quickly. Don't let them boss you around here, I know one of the governors, he's on our local Red Cross board, perhaps he could drop in to see you and make sure they're doing their stuff.' She leaned forward and kissed me on the forehead, then picked up her glasses and put them in her handbag. She waved good-bye and nearly walked into Alec's bed, then started off towards the ward toilets. A nurse came up and directed her towards the swing doors. By pure luck she found them and swept through. I felt mentally exhausted.

Gladys came over and examined my array of bottles. 'My! Aren't we lucky! D'you want some vinaigrette with that avocado?'

It was cruel. I had eaten nothing for ten days and had been looking forward to a few spoonfuls of consommé.

'Go take some Little Liver Pills,' I told her grumpily, 'you're a sadistic monster!' She giggled and started to gather up the various jars and bottles.

'I'll put them in the fridge for you, till you feel more like it. You'll never guess who's on his way up!'

'Santa Claus? Andy Williams? Robert Redford?'

She sighed theatrically. 'I wish he was! No, it's that awful Scotsman who was supposed to return to Glasgow. It seems he was taken to the train and put on it, then got off at the first stop and bummed his way back to London, sold his ticket, and has been on a binge ever since. Now he's carefully cut his wrists again to get back into the hospital!'

I only half-believed her story until a few minutes later a gurney was rolled into the ward and Jock, which became his inevitable name to Alec, sat up and gave us a thumbs-up sign with his bandaged hands. He was put into a vacant bed and sat there, grinning at everyone and giving cheek to the nurses.

'I ken ye're bonnie lassies and the food isna bad, so I'll rest here for a week or twa. I'm nae bother. Have ye got the lunch menu?'

A few minutes later a furious Dr Payne came in. He towered over the little Scotsman as if he could have throttled him. 'Mr Andrews, this is not some sort of charity hotel open for your convenience! You're supposed to be back in Glasgow, what the hell are you doing here again?'

'Calm doon, laddie. Ma wrists got all slashed again, I'm verra ill and need medical attention. I'm signed in doonstairs official-like an' I'll trouble ye to speak with respect to your elders!'

The doctor controlled his voice with an effort. 'Mr Andrews, try to understand one thing. It's only by sheer good luck that you haven't severed an artery in your wrists. You could have bled to death before you got here. It's no joking matter!'

Jock regarded Dr Payne with bucolic affection. 'Aye, I ken that. It's sorta like Russian roulette, that's wha' makes it so interesting. Could ye suggest some way to get in here that's a wee bit safer?'

I thought the psychiatrist would explode. Abruptly he turned and crossed to Mr Perry's bed. His face softened as he read the old man's chart. Mr Perry had been quiet all morning, and was actually thumbing through a magazine.

'A nice day, Mr P., feeling better?'

Mr Perry was entirely free, except for the leather cable

round his neck, loosely attached to the top of the bed. He looked up at the doctor with scared eyes.

'Yes, sir. When can I go home?'

'Soon, now, but let's not rush it. We want you to be fit and well again. Did you enjoy your birthday?'

Mr Perry nodded slowly, as if thinking again of what must have seemed like a miracle. Dr Payne waved at me and left the ward.

Lunch arrived and I was given a bowl of some thick cream soup. I ate it voraciously, although it had no salt and again tasted of nothing. After a few spoonfuls I found to my surprise I felt completely full. Bossy Boots passed by and took the plate away.

'Don't overdo it. Your stomach has severely contracted. Dr Marshall will be along soon to give you a spinal.'

I didn't like the sound of that. 'What's a spinal? I thought I was all finished with tests?'

'It's nothing much. She wants to take some marrow from your spinal cord. It's routine to make sure there's no after-effects from the poison.'

For the next hour my optimistic mood deteriorated rapidly. In novels I had read of spinal injections and how they could go wrong. By the time Dr Marshall arrived with two strange nurses I was a quaking bundle of nerves. My condition was not helped when the nurses fixed gauze masks over their faces. Dr Marshall tried to reassure me.

'It's not too bad! The main thing is that I want you to keep absolutely still while I'm doing it. It's important the needle goes in the right place.' It didn't reassure me at all.

I was turned on my side and told to draw up my legs as tightly as possible, whereupon a nurse wedged herself against my knees and clamped strong arms round my legs. I heard a trolley of instruments being wheeled across and muffled instructions given. The other nurse then held my shoulders in what felt like a judo grip.

'I'm going to start now,' said my tormentor's voice behind me. 'I have to go in very slowly. It won't hurt much but it doesn't feel very pleasant.'

It didn't. I winced as the needle entered my back, but there was little chance of moving with two stalwart nurses on top of me. Surprisingly, there wasn't much pain but I could feel that awful needle going steadily into my spine.

'Doing fine,' said Dr Marshall cheerily, 'just keep very, very still.'

I tried to think of something else and ignore that needle sinking deeper into me. I concentrated on the final scene of *Misty Horizon* – how did it go? – 'There is escape for none of us, we are all here, destined to die forever.' Great stuff, all I needed to cheer me up. I thought of the latest joke going around the clubs. A package is delivered bearing the inscription PHOTOS DO NOT BEND, and underneath the postman had written OH YES THEY DO! I had an awful desire to laugh, which was wiped out by an excruciating stab of pain up my back. The nurses tightened their grip.

'That's it, almost over! You've been very good. Just bear with me for a little longer.'

Soon it was over and the nurses released me. I lay under the covers completely exhausted. Dr Marshall patted me cheerfully.

'I wish they were all like you. If you feel like it, you can get up and sit in a chair this afternoon; you mustn't get too weak.'

'Weak?' I groaned. 'I feel as if I've been through a mangle. Will I ever recover?'

'Probably. You'll be pleased to hear your blood tests are excellent and there's almost no trace of poison. In a few days you'll be running round the ward!'

I didn't share her optimism.

With all the comings and goings I had lost touch with the other inmates of the ward. There was nice Mr Carstairs, who had dislocated his shoulders hanging from a balcony; there was the preacher with the cut throat; the little Scotsman, Mr Perry, and of course Alec. There seemed to be another burn case, who must have come in during the night, and who was lying motionless under a mountainous basket frame. Across the room King Kong had all day appeared to be under sedation. There were two beds empty at the bottom of the ward, and a new patient had been brought in while I was having my spinal and had been deposited across from my bed. He was connected to a heart machine and I could see the fluorescent blips were barely pulsating. I could have heard the latest news from Alec, but I was too tired and I slept for a couple of hours.

The tea trolley was brought around by a nurse, reminding me of poor Mr Fenchurch's unfortunate death. He must have known he was insane, some small part of his twisted brain retaining enough reality to carry out the final act. I drank some revolting lukewarm tea and refused the offer of a sticky cake, my stomach was not yet ready for such delicacies. I was amused to see that Jock was happily guzzling his tea and a plate with three cakes. I wondered how long he would be allowed to stay this time.

A short time later the preacher made his rounds of the ward, speaking to the conscious patients. When he arrived at my bed he raised his hand in mock salute.

'*Moriturus te saluto!* I am leaving in an hour and would like to wish you happiness in the future, and go with God's will. Tomorrow I will be back with my parishioners and all will be well with the world!'

Despite his levity, I believed him. There was something infinitely sad about this man who had temporarily lost his faith, then found it again. He knew he was returning to agonizing suffering and final death, yet his mind was now at peace and I was certain he would face it with calmness. Even as he spoke I could sense the pain was barely being held under by the drugs.

'Good-bye,' I said, embarrassed – for what does one say in the circumstances? – 'let's hope a miracle happens. They say there's always hope for a cure.' It sounded trite and I wished I hadn't said it.

He smiled, radiantly. 'Of course! The Lord will decide for me, I am in His hands. Good-bye!'

He crossed to Alec and again I thought how busy God must be. I was not being blasphemous, but I've always been uneasy about the way so many people depend on God to sort out their lives for them. A doorman I've known, off and on, for twenty years had systematically filled in his football pools every week, never with any success. One day he hit the jackpot, not a big one, but it converted him to religion. God had done it for him, he declared to everyone, and I remember I had had an awful vision of God hastily going through Littlewood's selections to make sure the right teams won for my friend.

The swing doors opened and a patient was wheeled in. Gently he was lifted on to one of the vacant beds. His arms and legs were encased in heavy plaster, and more plaster encased his ribs and neck. An intern skilfully connected up I.V. tubes into his arteries. He lay there, deathly pale and unmoving. Within a few minutes, Alec had talked with a nurse and had the latest news.

'Not too good,' he reported in a whisper to me, 'careless bloke, jumped off the top of a building and landed on a car. Broken legs, broken arms, broken vertebrae and ribs. I wonder what the car looked like!'

Tessa, the coloured nurse, interrupted us. 'Sorry, but it's time you got up. I'll help you on to your feet and then you can sit in that armchair for half an hour.'

I didn't feel that energetic, but obediently I tried to sit up straight, although my chest still hurt. She pulled back the sheets and swung my legs on to the floor. They felt like rubber. When I tried to stand my balance gave way and I would have fallen over if she hadn't held me securely. She called another nurse, and they propped me upright. The room steadied and I tried a step forward. My leg seemed to have no connection with my brain and refused to co-ordinate, thumping down on to the floor like an artificial limb.

'Don't worry,' said Tessa brightly, 'you'll be fine in a minute or two.' I stood there, supported by the two girls, feeling extremely foolish. Eventually they urged me forward again, and I managed to take two steps towards the chair. They lowered me into it and tucked a blanket round me; I felt exhausted, I would never walk again.

'Slowly, slowly!' advised Tessa. 'Don't forget you've been lying flat for over ten days; it takes a little time.'

I sat there miserably for nearly an hour, my bottom hurting and my chest aching, wondering if I would ever recover. But to my surprise, when they returned me to my bed, my feet responded and I walked the few steps almost without help. But the security and comfort of my narrow cot had never felt so good.

The soup for dinner tasted much better, and I even devoured some sort of wobbly jelly, which I'd never liked even as a child. I had hardly finished when I was astonished to hear Mr Perry talking to me.

'Pssst! You think I can go home tomorrow? You heard anything?'

I replied in a suitably conspiratorial whisper.

'No idea! Did you ask anyone?'

'Nah.'

'Well, ask someone, they're your friends.'

'Don't have no friends. But I'm going home to me daughter! You heard, din' you? I can go back!'

'Yes, it'll be fine for you. But don't rush it, they may want you to stay a few more days.'

'But why? I've bin good. Done what they say. Why can't I go home now?' His toothless mouth puckered and he appeared to be about to cry. I was terrified that he would suddenly flare up and I would be responsible.

'Mr Perry, don't *worry*! You'll be home very soon and you'll forget all about this hospital. Do you like growing flowers?'

I said this as a way of diverting his attention, not wanting to become involved in his psychosis. He was sitting upright and occasionally he would lean forward and the rubber strap round his neck would tighten and pull him back, although he seemed not to notice it.

Flowers appeared to be the right answer. He leaned back slightly, more relaxed.

'Flowers? Roses? I grew the best. All those roses! Damask – Musk – Briar, the Rose of Sharon, St John's Wort, a colour imagined but unknown!' I listened in amazement as he rambled on. I couldn't hear everything, but obviously he was an expert. Then his voice died away, and he lay back, staring upwards as if lost in a world of his own. I turned round to Alec.

'How goes your problem? When will you leave here?'

He put down his book. 'In the words of the immortal song, *There's no tomorrow* ... I spend many hours during the night planning how I can knock myself off, either here, or when I get out. I'd prefer it to be here, less messy. But much more difficult. I admire old Fenchurch, he managed to cut his throat with a fork; with a fork, mind you! That takes guts!'

I wished I had not brought up the subject.

'Come on, Alec, it's not that bad, for Christ's sake! There's a helluva lot you can do in life without playing football. Have you no other ambitions?'

For the first time I sensed the rage and despair beneath his outward profile.

'NO! No other ambition! Since I was nine years old I've played football, lived football, failed my exams because of football! I'm a League player, worth a small fortune! Until – until—' He closed his eyes, then glared at me. 'Now I'm useless; a has-been, a helpless cripple. The glamour's over, the shouting's died! Maybe I could get a job as a linesman, but even they have to run! Maybe I could sell programmes for my old club. No thanks! Football's the only thing I can do, the only thing I care about. I'm not going to get some bloody job as a clerk adding up figures.'

'So stay in that business! Couldn't you get a job on radio or television as a commentator? One has to know the ins and outs of the game pretty thoroughly. Maybe I could help you with introductions. I know a lot of fairly high-up boys in television.'

For a moment he showed a spark of interest, then he shrugged and turned back to his book. 'So what? There's a queue a mile long of ex-players, just as expert as I am. I'd never have a chance.'

'But try it, man!' I exclaimed in exasperation. 'They *might* just prefer you! If you don't try how the hell will you ever know? You're giving up far too easily!' Immediately I felt sorry, I could see he was fighting back tears. 'Alec, I mean it, when we get out of here I'll arrange some interviews for you, maybe it could work.'

When dinner arrived, Bossy Boots brought over a special tray for me. I realized I was again hungry, and was somewhat disgusted to see that all I was to be allowed was a plate of clear soup and a single boiled egg. She put the bed-tray on the floor while she helped me sit upright, then placed it over my knees.

'There! Can you manage to crack the egg yourself or should I help you? Have you drunk any water lately? My God it's a tough life!'

I was beginning to like her, despite her acid tongue and lack of charm. She was an indefatigable worker and obviously a very efficient nurse.

'You call that dinner?' I replied sullenly. 'It wouldn't satisfy a stuffed mouse!'

'Stuffed mice do not eat soup,' she snapped. 'I bet you don't even finish it, Bigmouth.'

She was almost right. My stomach was so contracted that even the bowl of soup was an effort. It took me a further ten minutes to eat the egg; I felt as if I had digested a four-course meal.

When the night staff came on, I looked in vain for the lovely Rhoda. There was a new nurse, a petite girl who I thought was Siamese, who came over and took my blood pressure and temperature, the usual two-hourly routine. She had shining black hair caught in a pony-tail. Her hands were tiny and delicate. She worked with swift precision. I asked her where Rhoda was.

'Her night off,' she replied in a soft sing-song voice. 'Me

Miss Lin, not as pretty as Rhoda, no? Everybody in love with her, she very nice lady.'

'You very nice lady, too! I haven't seen you before.'

'No, I have holiday, two lovely weeks. Now stay on night duty for next two weeks.'

I wanted to ask her how she came to be a qualified nurse in a big London hospital, but she gave me a flashing smile and departed on her rounds. I wondered what Rhoda was doing, feeling an absurd pang of jealousy as I imagined her at the theatre, glamorously robed, with some attractive young man at her side. She would have on a long white Grecian dress, with a simple gold belt, and her red hair would spill seductively down her back. Her thoughts would be far from the sordid Graveyard ward.

Well, one can dream, can't one?

I had fallen into an uneasy sleep and was having confused nightmares about the production of *Misty Horizon*; everything seemed to be going wrong. A stunt man had jumped off the top of a building and nothing had been placed below to break his fall. He was lying in a squashed mess of blood and bone and I was desperately trying to find a reason not to go near him, knowing myself to be a coward. Nobody else seemed to have noticed and they were shooting the scene again with another stuntman. I wanted to yell out, but the second man jumped and he too crashed to the ground.

I became aware of a dry coughing sound, a choking sob which impinged on my dream. I opened my eyes and heard the usual familiar sounds of the ward. It must have been the middle of the night as there were few nurses around.

I turned over and found myself staring at Mr Perry's bed. For a moment, in the dim light, I didn't comprehend what was happening. Then I saw the old man was hanging downwards over the side of the bed, supported only by the strap round his neck. His face was purple and he was strangling.

Without thinking I threw back the sheet and lunged towards him. My balance and weakness took over and I crashed to the floor, but managed to get hold of his shoulders and support him. Immediately warning buzzers sounded, and two startled nurses came running over.

I must have blacked out for a few seconds, because I became aware I was back in bed, my heart beating like a frenzied samba and one knee hurting like hell. Miss Sims was sponging my forehead. 'Is he all right?' I asked faintly. 'He was choking to death!'

'He'll be all right, thanks to you. Will you stop being the hero and let *us* look after the patients? Are you all right?'

'I think so. My knee hurts a bit, I fell on it.'

She pulled back the sheet and examined it, probing and testing. 'Nothing broken, just a nasty bruise. We'll see how it is in the morning. Will you try to sleep?'

Perchance to dream. But I agreed. My enforced activity had left me limp. I turned over and saw they had an oxygen mask on Mr Perry, and he was now under a restraining sheet. 'They won't punish him?' I asked Miss Sims.

'That's up to Dr Payne, but it's his own fault,' she said unsympathetically, 'he knows he's absolutely forbidden to get out of bed.'

I felt sad for Mr Perry. He had broken his 'parole', for whatever reason, and could be back to square one.

I dozed off. The next thing I heard was a low sharp whistle. In a fright, I opened my eyes and peered cautiously around. I felt a wave of terror as I saw there were no nurses in the ward except the one bent over the control board. In a moment the swing doors opened and a white-jacketed figure came in, silently and swiftly. He crossed over to King Kong's bed for a few seconds and bent over the still figure. The man's back was towards me and the ward had little light apart from a spotlight over the control centre.

The man straightened up and swiftly left the ward. In both cases he had ignored the nurse on the board, and she had not looked up. A moment later the whistle, short and sharp, sounded again, and several nurses entered from the rest-room at the other end of the ward.

I lay still, my eyes almost closed, pretending to be asleep, dreading any developments. I felt my heart pound again when a few minutes later two attendants wheeled in a gurney and stopped beside King Kong's bed. With difficulty they moved the inert figure on to the trolley, covering it with a sheet, and silently departed.

Had Jim Danvers been right? Had I just witnessed another case of euthanasia, or was I hallucinating again, or was it all a bad dream? I shrank deeper under the sheet to give myself more protection.

Sleep eluded me, but eventually I entered the arms of Morpheus, because I remember having more nightmares, confused dreams of high buildings and an assassin following me, a faceless shadow I knew was there but who never came close enough to be seen. Then I was awake again and watching the pale shades of dawn driving back the terrors of the night.

Miss Lin noticed I was not asleep and at five o'clock brought a cup of tea from the nurses' rest-room. I sat up and leaned against the extra pillows she gave me, and I noticed that my chest and throat were less painful, although my knee was tender and throbbing. As the daylight brightened, I tried to ridicule my fears of the long night; it was absurd even to imagine that patients were conveniently dispatched by some ghoulish gentleman who stole into the ward to carry out his dreadful mission.

But King Kong's bed was empty and flat, neatly made up to receive the next mutilated guest. When Miss Lin came to collect my cup I asked her casually what had happened to him.

'His heart gave out. Poor man, he had body of a giant but brain of a child. Perhaps it better this way, he very unhappy all his life.'

'Tell me, I've occasionally heard a short, sharp whistle during the night; what does it mean?'

She looked vague. 'A whistle? Perhaps it one of the machines. Lots of computers here, very efficient. You like to read a little?'

'But when it happens, there don't seem to be any nurses around. Isn't that a coincidence?'

She smiled, her perfect teeth white in the innocent face. 'Sometimes is quiet in the ward, and nurses go for cup of tea. Very naughty, but girl always on duty at Control, and cameras watching all time!' The bland eyes seemed to be laughing at me as if I was an inquisitive child asking stupid questions.

Or was my imagination working overtime again?

As far as I could see, there were no new entries during the night and, apart from King Kong, no one had departed. In the bed on the other side of Alec, who was still asleep, I could see the chap who had jumped off the building and landed on a car. He was awake and caught my glance. He raised one of his plastered arms an inch or two in greeting. I waved back, wondering what his thoughts must be.

I tried to imagine what his last moments must have been as he hurled himself from the top of the building, a few seconds of eternity as he fell, still conscious with the knowledge that he had taken the irrevocable step, the remorseless ground rushing up at an incredible speed, the smashing impact as he hit the roof of the car parked below. Then the awful return to gradual consciousness, slowly aware of his aliveness, the brain still trapped in the smashed body; nothing solved and even more problems to face, his mind gripped in pain-memory.

By eight o'clock the ward had been wakened, washed, fed, and charts filled in, and the day staff was filtering in. I had eaten some thin porridge, which normally I detested, but which tasted remarkably good to my deprived palate. Ten days without smoking or drinking can restore both taste and smell to an astonishing degree.

Dr Marshall arrived, elegant as ever, cheerful as usual.

'You can try to walk around today. One of the nurses will help you. Don't try too much at a time, just once round the ward. If you feel too exhausted get straight back into bed. I've made an appointment for you to see Mr Garold, the ear specialist, at three o'clock. Meanwhile I'm putting you on a high vitamin course. You'll have to swallow three spansules every two hours. The poison's just about gone and we've got to build up your strength now.'

It was good news, as subconsciously I had been dreading another relapse and having Mr Jordan chatting to me again.

'What happened to my marrow-bone operation? I hope that's all finished with.'

She laughed. 'All clear! You're a very healthy specimen. Now let's have a look at your knee, I hear you were doing acrobatics last night.'

She examined my sore knee. It was slightly skinned and had a huge blue bruise round it. I winced when she manipulated it. 'We'll put on some medication, but it's only a bad contusion. I think you're a masochist, haven't you got enough sores?'

She called over Gladys and gave some instructions, then I had to turn on my stomach while Gladys took the dressing off my bottom for Dr Marshall to examine.

'My!' she said bright. 'It's turned a beautiful sunset colour! Anyway, it's a good sign, it's starting to heal nicely.'

Dr Payne came in shortly after Dr Marshall had departed. He was with the Floor Matron and he strode up to Mr Perry's bed and regarded him balefully. The little man, still under a restraining sheet, looked tiny and pathetic lying there with only his face visible.

'I think you're a wicked old man,' Dr Payne said finally, 'but Matron wants me to give you another chance. Why did you try to get out of bed?'

There was a long pause, then Mr Perry spoke faintly. 'I was trying to go home. I want to go home!'

'*I'll* decide when you go home! D'you realize you might have been dead if your friend here hadn't saved you? What d'you think of that? He got out of bed to save you from strangling, you ungrateful, evil man!'

I knew this was rubbish. The alarm had rung almost at the same time I had leapt up; I supposed the doctor was using his usual cunning approach.

Mr Perry slowly turned his head and looked at me. I smiled and waved at him. He regarded me solemnly. 'You saved my life!' he said in wonder, as if only now taking in the fact.

'All right, Matron,' boomed Dr Payne, 'we'll give wicked old Mr Perry another chance. Nurse, take that sheet off him!'

Bossy Boots came up and undid the restraining sheet, putting an extra pillow behind him and helping him to sit up. She handled him like a recalcitrant baby, and while she was making him comfortable he kept staring at me.

Dr Payne leant over him until their faces were only inches apart. 'Just remember one thing, wicked old Mr Perry! You try getting out of bed again before I tell you, and next time we'll let you hang yourself! Clear?'

I suppose Dr Payne's therapy was justified, but I felt intensely sorry for the old man. Even at the best of times a layman is afraid of the all-knowing doctor, but when one is ill and in hospital one feels completely in their power and akin to some ignorant prisoner, totally submissive to their whims and orders. Mr Perry was obviously terrified of anyone in authority.

Shortly afterwards, Bossy Boots came across and held out my dressing-gown. 'Time for walkies. Can you get out of bed by yourself? Try it!'

Obediently, I slid my legs to the floor and stood up slowly and groggily while she helped me into the robe. She handed me a walking-stick and took my other arm. I would have preferred a more glamorous nurse to be holding me, but there was something reassuring about this woman's strength. We started slowly shuffling round the room.

Now I had a chance to see the other patients more closely. I tried not to appear too interested, a natural shyness not to probe into other people's afflictions. Alec gave me a thumbs-up sign, grinning. The next patient, the man who had fallen on the car, gave a cracked grin, then winced in pain as he tried to move an arm. It felt strange to be upright again, actually walking, if somewhat unsteadily, but I longed for the safety and security of my bed, now several yards away.

I had a momentary shock as we passed the burn case at the end of the ward. From my bed, I had only been able to see the high wicker frame which had been placed over his body to keep the bedsheet clear. Now I saw his face, a bright splotch of raw red flesh, the lips black and twisted, the hair frizzled away. His eyes were open but staring unseeingly at the ceiling. I wondered if he would ever look normal again.

Another patient, who had been brought in the previous day and wired to a heart machine, was sitting up reading a newspaper. His wrists were heavily bandaged, but he put down his paper and wished me good-morning in a strong authoritative voice. He wore a pince-nez and seemed a most healthy specimen; again I marvelled to what depths of despair a man must sink to want to take his own life. Then I realized that I, too, probably evoked the same thought in other people.

We stopped by Mr Carstair's bed. He had a kind, gentle face but wrinkled like a prune, and I guessed his age to be in the middle fifties. I remembered he was the man who had thrown himself off his apartment balcony, then managed to hold on, breaking his collar bones. He spoke in a well-modulated, educated voice.

'Feeling better today? You must be glad to get out of bed!'

I replied truthfully. 'I feel like hell! But, yes, it's good to be on my feet again.' I noticed Mr Carstairs was still hooked up to a heart machine, which seemed to be pulsing erratically. His face was very white and I remembered he had a heart problem as well as his other injuries.

We passed another patient lying very still and unconscious, then came to the Scotsman's bed. Needless to say, he was sitting up and watching the goings-on in the ward with bright bird-like eyes. He greeted me like an old friend.

'Watch yersel', laddie! Dinna get well too soon or they'll

throw yer oot. Nurse, could a body get a wee drop o' whisky roon here? Just as medicine for ma heart, ye ken!'

'I'll give you a wee drop of arsenic!' said Bossy Boots, urging me slowly past the bed. 'You've got the cheek of the devil, coming back here!'

Jock cackled delightedly. 'Ye're a bonnie lassie, mebbe ye'll come up a dark alley wi' me one day!'

'Sure, with a sledgehammer!' snapped back my nurse, then we were at the next bed, where a man lay motionless, rubber tubes snaking up his nose and some sort of gag between his teeth. An oxygen cylinder and mask stood beside the bed. He, too, was attached to a heart monitor, and the green blips were ominously flat, pulsating only very slightly.

'What happened to him?' I asked in a whisper. 'I don't remember him coming in.'

'He was brought in yesterday, probably while you were dozing. He has terminal cancer and his wife tried to give him a massive dose of pain-killers, then regretted it and called for an ambulance. Poor bastard, it would have been kinder to let him go.'

We walked on slowly; I was beginning to feel stronger although my balance was rotten. Perhaps I had hoped for a miracle, that I would rise from my death-bed, cured.

'Tell me, doesn't it depress you terribly to see all these cases coming in, day after day, most of them scarred for the rest of their lives. Wouldn't most of them be better off dead?'

She looked up at me through her ugly, heavy-lensed glasses. 'At first I hated it. I suppose I still do, but now it's just a job of nursing and I don't let myself get too involved. Sure, it's depressing, because for every failure that comes in here, there's another one out there who succeeded. But that's part of the price we pay for a so-called civilized world. The strong will succeed and the misfits will drop by the way.' She squeezed my arm as if in apology. 'I don't mean you. You're a little different. I'm sure if you'd been happily married or had children or parents you'd never have considered suicide.'

I was surprised at her knowledge of my background and her acute perception. 'Yes,' she went on, steering me back towards my bed, 'most of them would certainly be better off dead. "By the waters of Babylon we sat down and wept!" We struggle to keep them alive, despite themselves, in order that they can be tortured a while longer. Sometimes it seems crazy.'

After she had tucked me into bed her professional manner returned. 'See you drink plenty of water or juice,' she commanded. 'Oh yes! Your bowels will start to work now, so don't be shy about asking for a bedpan!' She grinned maliciously and stalked away.

'No chance,' I called after her, 'I'll make it to the loo if it kills me!' Not a very appropriate remark, I thought afterwards.

I felt quite proud of my walk round the ward, although it was a relief to sink back on my pillows. I noticed Alec's bed was empty, and wondered if he had been taken to fit his artificial feet. I turned to Mr Perry, who again was regarding me with something like awe.

'Hi, Mr Perry! You feeling fine?'

For the first time his toothless mouth cracked open in the semblance of a smile.

'Yes thank you . . . you saved my life!'

'Nonsense, the nurses were coming to help you anyway. Just don't fall out of bed again!'

'But I'm going home! You heard my daughter yesterday! I'm going home! I promise I'll be good now, I was just lonely, they told me they didn't want me anymore.'

I tried to soothe him, afraid he would jump out of bed and commit hara-kiri again. 'Sure you're going home, but you've got to get your strength back first. You saw how weak I was just now, and you've been in bed longer than I have. Just wait till Dr Payne says it's okay.'

A gurney was wheeled through the swing doors and a still figure was gently deposited on the bed beyond Mr Perry. Two nurses connected up intravenous pipes and taped the sticky metal lodes to his chest to convey his heartbeats to the omniscient heart machine. He looked quite young, but his face was marble white. A doctor came in and talked briefly with the Sister in charge, a nice woman whose name I didn't know. I saw him briefly shake his head and caught the words '... massive brain damage ...'

Alec was brought back in a wheelchair, looking slightly more cheerful than on his last outing. He was helped into bed and turned to me.

'My new feet are much more comfortable! I even staggered round the fitting room. Maybe I'll play football again yet!'

At ten minutes to three my friend Fred arrived with his wheelchair. I was tucked in and we set off for my appointment with Mr Garold. Again, we made a bewildering journey along lengthy corridors. Finally I was deposited in a small waiting-room, discreetly marked 'Mr E. G. Garold'. I've often wondered why specialists and surgeons are always 'Mr' and never 'Dr', although I believe it dates back over two hundred years and involved a kind of inverted snobbery when surgeons considered themselves vastly superior to the so-called doctors of the day.

A cheerful intern came and took my blood pressure, then wheeled me into a small operating theatre. He and a nurse helped me on to the table and told me to relax and lie flat.

'I have to run a test on you first,' he announced, 'it's not very pleasant but it won't take long. Now look straight up at the ceiling. You see that black cross?'

Directly above my head was a small black cross painted on the white ceiling. 'My eyes are fine,' I said with rare humour, 'it's my ears I'm worried about!'

'Don't knock it,' he smiled, 'your balance problem can also stem from your eyes. We have to ascertain that it *was* your ear operation which caused the imbalance. Now, I'm going to syringe each ear with a fine condensed jet, first with hot water, then with cold, half a minute of each. The worst part is the noise, it'll sound like a bloody waterfall. I want you to shut your eyes while I'm doing this. The moment it stops, open your eyes and look straight up at that cross. Then just tell me if you can see it clearly, and whether it moves or not. Understand?'

The nurse inserted some sort of nozzle in my right ear, and I closed my eyes. She held it gently but firmly against my head, and I waited without enthusiasm for the water.

Next moment the world seemed to fall on me. The compressed water roared and thundered against my eardrum, unpleasantly hot, deafening me with its cataclysmic clamour. I could feel the water trickling wetly down my cheek into a plastic gutter on the edge of the table.

Abruptly it stopped. I opened my eyes and looked at the black cross. 'Well?' the intern asked.

'It's still there, quite clear.'

'Good. Now for the cold water.' Again the smashing impact of noise, this time unpleasantly cold water. Again the same question and answer. Then the nurse transferred the tube to my other ear. I winced as the jet of sound penetrated my ear. Thankfully I felt it stop and opened my eyes.

The black cross was now a blob, moving rapidly away to the right. Try as I could I was unable to focus on it. I tried to sit up but the room spun round. Gently the nurse pushed me back. Her face was blurred and the walls seemed to be falling on top of me.

'I think that's all we need,' the intern said quietly, 'I won't do the cold water. Just lie there for a couple of minutes and your sight will return to normal. When you're ready I'll take you in to see Mr Garold.'

It was five minutes before I felt well enough to sit up. The nurse tucked me into the wheelchair and we went through into a large office, furnished like a comfortable library. An oldish man with a grey beard and heavy glasses arose from behind a handsome Sheraton desk. Without any greeting he came round and stood in front of me. The intern came in with some papers and handed them to Mr Garold, who examined them briefly.

'Dr Walters, help the patient to his feet and hold him steady.' With difficulty, I climbed out of the chair, the nurse and intern helping me. 'Now. Place your feet together and close your eyes. Don't worry, Dr Walters will hold you.'

I did as I was told and immediately fell sideways. Dr Walters caught me by the shoulders.

'My dear sir,' said Mr Garold smugly, 'you have a balance problem.'

I could cheerfully have murdered him.

Back in The Graveyard, I lay exhausted in bed, my ears still singing and my sight tending to blur. But now I could see the funny side of it, or perhaps I was light-headed. Mr Garold had asked many questions about my previous operation, obviously intrigued as to how the liquid in the middle ear had been displaced. It all added up to a big zero. I waited for him to say the magic words that I would learn to live with it.

'A very interesting case,' he had intoned, 'most unusual and unfortunate. Not the surgeon's fault, of course.' (Of course not, it never is. Probably mine, for having funny ears.) 'I'm afraid there's little one can do, we're not magicians, you know, and what's done is done. However, as time passes you'll learn to live with it.'

Mr Garold may have been a brilliant E.N.T. specialist, but he had as much charm as a thick fog on a rainy day. However, it was most reassuring to know I would learn to live with it. I'd jolly well have to.

Vaguely I noticed a large woman enter the ward, dressed in outdoor clothes. She was obviously a visitor, and she eyed the room imperiously before crossing to the patient with the broken arms and legs who had landed on a car. Alec leaned over towards me and asked how my test had been. It was amazing how he seemed to know everything that was going on.

'Not too good,' I admitted, 'there's nothing I can do about this imbalance. But no doubt I'll grow to like it! How about you, have you decided life may still be worth living?'

'Can't say yet. Maybe I'll go to live in Canada; at least I can't get frostbite in my toes!'

We both heard the raised voices at the bed next to Alec. I was just in time to see the woman give the man a swinging slap across the face, then she turned and marched out of the ward. The man started to cry, his useless arms jerking convulsively.

There was a shocked silence in the ward, as if we had seen something obscene, which indeed we had. Then Gladys and another nurse ran across and started to comfort the man. I felt sick and turned away, embarrassed for him and with a stabbing hatred for that awful woman, wondering what sort of mind could conceive hitting a desperately ill man who could hardly move.

'No wonder he jumped off a building,' remarked Alec, who never seemed fazed by anything, 'fancy living with that old bitch!' But for once I couldn't laugh, the incident had been too nauseating.

In the late afternoon I had a visit from Josh, my assistant. Despite his efforts to be jocular, he was ill-at-ease and hardly stopped talking. It was a relief when he left, but I was glad in some ways, as I had not felt any embarrassment, which seemed a good sign for when I had to face the outside world again. In fact, despite Mr Garold's gloomy predictions, I was feeling much better, and when Rhoda came on duty I greeted her like a long-lost lover.

She came over to see me almost immediately, her smile radiant and her long red hair piled magnificently on top of her head, the tiny cap perched precariously high. She examined the chart at the end of my bed and nodded encouragingly.

'You seem in fine fettle! You ran round the ward today!'

'Only in frustration because you weren't here! Now my day is made, come and soothe my fevered brow.' Instead, she stuck a thermometer in my mouth and took my pulse.

'Huh! Disgustingly normal! I'm offended. Have you opened your bowels yet?'

I looked at her in mock horror. 'You insensitive wench, how can you talk of such sordid things when we should be looking at the moon and mouthing pretty nothings! Where is your soul? Your sense of romance? Shall I not call upon thy loveliness to sustain my ardour? "You walk in beauty like the night, of cloudy climes and starry skies, and all that's best of dark and bright, meet in your aspect and your eyes!"'

'Wow,' she breathed, clutching her bosom. 'I repeat, have you had a bowel movement today?'

'Definitely no heart can beat below that sexy uniform,' I muttered darkly. 'No, I have not been to the loo.'

'Perhaps an enema would help,' she said sweetly. 'I love giving enemas, especially to romantic swains!'

Perhaps it was the power of suggestion, or the fear of an enema, but an hour later I had the urge. Rhoda was busy with a patient, so I signalled Gladys, who was still on duty.

'Gladys, I want to go to the toilet. Can you help me there?' She looked dubious.

'Wouldn't you prefer a bedpan?'

'No thanks. I feel fine. Just give me a hand to the bathroom.' I slid carefully out of bed before she could argue. She handed me my stick and we made slow progress to the end of the ward where the baths and lavatories were situated.

She propped me up against a wall while she put down an antiseptic cover on the toilet. 'Try not to sit on your right cheek, otherwise you'll disturb the dressing. I'll wait for you outside. There's no need to lock the door, I have a master key anyway!'

It was painful sitting on the seat, and after a minute of listening to Gladys humming a tune outside the door, I no longer had the urge. Furious, I stood up and retied my dressing-gown.

'That was quick,' Gladys joked as I opened the door, 'did everything come out all right in the end?'

'Very funny. I'm beginning to think you nurses ought to be on at the Palladium. Unfeeling broads!'

We had just returned to the ward when the urge overtook me again. Imbalance or not, I made record time back to the loo, this time with great success. When I returned to bed Rhoda passed by.

'Hey,' I said smugly, 'you know what you can do with your enema!'

I thought it was quite a clever remark.

As darkness crept in that evening, I noticed the distant roofs of the buildings had disappeared in a thick mist. It was raining too, and I thought of the outside world hurrying miserably about its business, raincoats buttoned up, drivers cursing as traffic jams built up; and here I was, warm and protected in my hospital cocoon.

It was about eleven o'clock and the ward had settled down to its uneasy sleep when I became aware of unusual activity among the nurses. Not being too tired, I sat up and watched as more overhead lights were turned on, and extra nurses appeared through the swing doors. Six narrow camp beds were brought in and placed cross-wise at the foot of some of the existing ones, then covered with sheets and pillows. Extra oxygen cylinders were wheeled in and portable trolleys containing bottles, tubes, and instruments were rolled into position. All this was accomplished almost in silence as most of the patients slept on.

Miss Sims, the black Sister, paused by my bed as she noticed I was sitting up.

'What's the panic?' I asked in a whisper. 'It looks like there's a war on!'

She smiled briefly. 'There is, in a way. There's been a massive pile-up on the motorway, about thirty cars and buses involved. It always happens when there's fog, people just won't slow down. We're taking in most of the casualties, even though we're full. Some of the overflow will come in here. If I were you I'd try to sleep, it won't be a pleasant sight!'

She hurried off. Intrigued, I watched the systematic preparations, marvelling at the organization and calmness which prevailed, each intern and nurse seemed to have a specific duty to carry out.

I heard the ambulances in the distance, but the sirens always cut out near the hospital to avoid disturbing patients. I snuggled down in bed, not wishing to appear morbidly curious, which I was. It is a sad but true reflection on human nature that accidents of any kind, from an aircraft crash to a trapeze act falling, attract onlookers like flies.

Twenty minutes later the first victims were wheeled in. At first I thought the leading gurney contained a child, until I saw it was a female with no legs. In the emergency reception downstairs they had cut away her dress, and the lower part of her torso was covered in bloodstained dressings. The second trolley contained a man whose face was a red mushy blob, and even from my bed I could see shards of glass sticking out of it. I had seen enough. I lay back and looked at the ceiling, listening to the moans of agony which now filled the ward, despite the morphine and sedation which had been administered in the ambulances.

Already there were doctors and interns working on the new patients. I presumed the operating theatres and emergency rooms were already full. I looked again and saw an attractive blonde girl being helped off a gurney. She was dazed but conscious, her green evening dress ripped and covered in mud. She had a long gash down the side of her cheek, but otherwise seemed unhurt. One of the 'lucky' ones.

In the middle of all this organized chaos the alarm buzzer sounded over Mr Carstair's bed. I looked across and saw the green pulse almost flat. In a moment nurses were beside him, administering injections. I found myself holding my breath until the blips increased.

I noticed the woman without legs had not been attended

to, nor had they connected up the usual drip lines. I realized why, a short time after, when an intern bent over briefly and felt for a heartbeat. He signalled to one of the gurney attendants and she was lifted on to a trolley and covered with a sheet, then wheeled out. Death had been kind to her.

I lay back again and thought of all the sadness and suffering the night had brought, only through careless driving and the first unfortunate accident. The motorway blocked, perhaps not even a serious mishap, but the vehicles behind, blundering too fast through fog, smashing relentlessly into one another, pile-up after pile-up, death and destruction and blood and torn flesh, minute after terrible minute before one of the uninjured could run back far enough to slow the oncoming traffic. I remembered being in Hollywood a few years before when a similar crash happened on the freeway near Malibu, when an incredible hundred and sixty-two cars piled into one another at high speed.

Now tonight, overflowing into our ward, were patients who had no intention of committing suicide, victims who an hour or so ago had been happily returning home, going to a party, an amorous date, a theatre, or just returning from a Bingo hall. Talking, chatting, discussing, perhaps swearing at the rain and fog, never dreaming it was to be a night they would remember for the rest of their lives; provided they were still alive.

Eventually I must have slept, for it was nearly seven when a gentle hand shook me awake. It was Rhoda, for once looking tired and strained. Her usually crisp uniform had ugly red marks on it, and wisps of hair were falling out from her well-coiffured head.

'Time to wake up! Here's your tea and I'll be back with soap and water in a minute.'

I sat up and saw that all but two of the emergency beds had been removed. The trolleys and gurneys and cylinders had vanished, and The Graveyard was its normal ship-shape self. When Rhoda returned I asked her how it had been accomplished.

'They used this ward as a temporary clearing station until

we could allocate spare beds in other wards. In a big hospital like this there's a lot of red tape and paperwork, and the emergency reception theatres were too full to cope with the injured, so they were sent up here to have preliminary treatment. By around five nearly everyone had been placed in other wards.'

'How many injured were there?'

'I've no idea. Some were taken to other hospitals, but we coped with about seventy cases here.'

It had been a night of carnage and slaughter, all needless. Our suicide ward and its problems seemed very small.

By midday the ward had returned to what might be termed 'normal', the last two accident cases having been removed. I had talked with Mr Perry, who seemed much more relaxed and even anxious to carry on a conversation. I started to read an Irwin Shaw paperback which Alec had lent me, when the swing doors opened and my wife Gloria entered.

She caused quite a sensation. An attractive blonde, she was wearing a black Dior trouser suit with gold buttons, which fitted her slim figure to perfection. Alec gave a low whistle which he changed to a cough as she came over to my bed. She was carrying a large azalea plant. She was almost as embarrassed as I was.

She put down the plant and sat on the edge of my bed. For no reason at all I felt tears very close.

'Hullo.'

'Hullo.'

'Thought I'd bring you this plant, you always liked them. Can I smoke in here?'

'Yes. There's an ashtray on the table. You're looking well.'

'Thanks. So are you. I expected to find a pale ghost!'

'It's a lovely plant. Thank you for coming.'

She talked rapidly, blowing out a long plume of cigarette smoke. 'I should have come yesterday, but I had so much to do. Mother said you seemed fine. How's the food here, do they look after you?'

'Yes, very well. I've only just started eating, even a plate of soup fills me up. But I'm allowed up now; I walked right round the ward yesterday.'

'That's great. You don't mind being in a ward?'

'No. There's lots of attractive nurses, all waiting for me to lay them when I get out.'

'So they should! I hope you're not using the casting-couch line.'

A long pause.

'How's Derek?' Derek was her new boyfriend.

'He's fine. He'd have liked to come up, but felt it wasn't very proper. Are you very unhappy?'

'Not any longer. I suppose it was a silly thing to do, but it seemed like a good idea at the time.'

'I felt so awful when I heard. Guilty, too. I've been an awful bitch.'

Again the tears felt near. I changed the subject.

'Forget it! What's done is done. We'll get an amicable divorce and I'll marry a rich old American heiress. Have you spoken to Josh or any of the office?'

'Yes, they've been very kind and tactful. I'm to report back to tell them how you are, and whether you want anyone to come and see you.'

'Not quite yet. In a few days I'll be ready to face up to things again; just now I'm trying to decide what to do with my new life, as you might call it.' Silence; we were two strangers.

'I'd better go. I promised the Sister down the hall I'd only stay a minute or two.' She stubbed out the cigarette with obvious relief. Her eyes were moist when she kissed me on the forehead. 'Take care of yourself, get well soon!'

After she had left, I could see the bewilderment on Alec's face. He leant over towards me. 'That dish is your *wife*? And you're in here? You *must* be nuts!'

'We're getting a divorce.'

He nodded knowingly.

'Ah! Now I get you. But no woman's worth doing yourself in. There's so many other fish in the sea!'

I didn't disillusion him. Let him think I had a broken

heart as well as a ropey balance. I could even see the funny side of it.

The patient who had been brought in the previous day and put in the bed next to Mr Perry had recovered consciousness. A doctor and two interns and Bossy Boots were clustered round the bedside. I watched curiously as they gently pulled him to a sitting position. He turned his head slowly and I winced inwardly.

Even with no knowledge of medicine I could see he was now an imbecile, a complete vegetable. He was quite young, in his early thirties, with what must have been a strong, intelligent face. But now the eyes were opaque and blank, not even focusing. His mouth hung open and a trickle of saliva ran down his chin. One of the interns uncovered his feet and pressed down on the toes, which I knew from Dr Marshall's examination to be highly painful. There was no reaction whatsoever from the man.

The doctor bent close to the patient's face and shone a pen-light in his eyes. Even as he did so the man's head slid sideways and remained so, like a rag doll. It was quite horrible to watch.

'You were lucky,' I heard Alec say. 'He took an overdose, too, but they obviously didn't find him in time. That poor bastard's brain's gone for ever.'

I felt numb, thinking how so easily that could have been me. Perhaps there was a God up there after all.

In the afternoon I was due for my walk, and a new nurse called Jerri came to help me. She was tall, with a plain, angular face, but she was a natural comic. She laughed constantly, as if everything in life was a huge joke. I wondered how much was simulated, or whether she covered up her own feelings by this built-in defence.

I was now feeling much stronger, and we walked up and down the ward twice. I learnt that Jerri was married with two children, but her husband made a good salary and they had a live-in au pair girl who looked after the kids.

'But don't you find the long hours difficult for your

married life? You must be exhausted by the end of the day?' I asked curiously.

The touch on my arm was light, she was letting me walk almost on my own. 'It's not too bad. Usually I work the relief middle shift, from nine till four, or I fill in for anyone who's ill or away.'

'How long have you been a nurse?'

'I started when I was eighteen,' she giggled girlishly, 'that's over fourteen years ago! I didn't want to give it up when I got married, I love it too much. Of course, I had to take a few months off when I had the brats. My husband thinks it's good for me to work, provided I'm home at nights. The hospital's very understanding, so everyone's happy.'

A patient had rung for a bedpan and the other nurses were busy. The Sister on the Control board signalled Jerri to attend to it. 'Can you manage on your own, or should I take you back to bed?' she asked me.

'I'll be all right. I have my stick.'

I crossed over slowly to Mr Carstairs. He was his usual cheerful self, despite the fact he was fighting for life with his weak heart. But at the moment his machine was pulsing healthily.

'I'm reading a marvellous book, if you'd like to borrow it later. About Africa and the tribal customs. Very quaint. Some of it sheer superstition, of course, but some of it makes a lot of sense. Listen to this: "Nothing must be left empty for the hereafter. Leave some soup in the platter, some wine in the gourd and some dignity in the human body, so that they go forward prepared." How about that!'

'A bit fancy for me,' I replied, unimpressed, 'but I suppose it's nice to know there'll be soup and wine in the hereafter!'

I would have liked to find out more about Mr Carstairs. Alec had said he was impotent, and obviously he also had a bad heart. But his speech and bearing were those of a highly intelligent man.

'I know it's none of my business, but what profession are you in? You can tell me to bugger off, of course!'

He laughed delightedly, trying not to move his broken

shoulders. 'My dear boy, we could play at Twenty Questions! No, better still, What's My Line. What do *you* think I do?'

He had put me on a spot. If I made too lowly a guess he could be offended. 'A banker,' I said brightly, 'someone important in the City!'

He liked that, but shook his head. 'How flattering you are. Try again.'

'I must have a clue. Do you help people?'

'You could say that.'

'A dental surgeon?' He shook his head.

'Connected with medicine?'

'No.'

'Insurance?'

'No.'

'Stock Exchange, a broker?'

'No, nowhere near. Try again.'

'Something physical?'

'Yes, that's better. Look, you must be getting tired, I don't think you'll ever guess. I'm a deep-sea diver, now an Inspector in charge of Thames Salvage. Or I *was*.'

We both laughed. It was incredible how wrong one can be to go by appearances.

I returned to bed, feeling pleased at my little walk. I was lying back thinking about Mr Carstairs when Dr Payne came in, followed by an orderly with a wheelchair. He came over to me.

'Sorry about the short notice, but Dr Strombold's just had a cancellation so I've fitted you in for a neurology test. You're to go straight down now.'

I was startled. 'What sort of test is that?' I didn't like the sound of it.

'Pure routine,' he said cheerfully. 'It's a computer which measures the brain's reactions to the eyes. We want to be sure your co-ordination hasn't been damaged. It won't hurt!'

So a minute later I was trundling down the corridors again, this time being pushed by a young man with a beard. On the way he told me about himself. He was studying for a degree in engineering, and during the holiday recess he worked in the hospital as an orderly. He had a wife who was a model, and a small child. He was a likeable fellow with a good sense of humour.

At a certain point he stopped to consult a map. 'I've only been at this hospital for two weeks, and I still get lost. I think we take this elevator to the third floor.'

We did. He wheeled me down a long corridor and through double doors marked MATERNITY. We backed out with some confusion and eventually found Neurology on the floor above.

Dr Strombold turned out to be an ominous-looking lady in her fifties. She sat me down in the middle of a large room which had banks of computers, control panels, and an unpleasant looking metal object, like a dentist's drill, except that the swinging arm had several cables with electrodes on the end. She had two assistants who were manning the controls and dials.

'Now, let me explain first what I'm about to do,' she said pleasantly, 'so that you don't think we're about to electrocute you. Five of these wires will be attached to your head with frozen acetate. These will feed the brain impulses into the computers. Then I'm going to give you various charts and coloured lights to look at. All you have to do is focus on them, the machine does the rest. The worst part of the whole operation is getting the electrodes off again, it makes a sticky mess!'

I still didn't like it but tried to show insouciance. 'If you pull them off, it'll be known as *The Wrench Connection* maybe?' She winced slightly, but smiled bravely. It really wasn't that funny.

She produced what looked like a classic instrument of torture. It was shaped like a crown, with five metal spikes. She parted my hair and I hoped I hadn't developed dandruff. It had now been over two weeks since I had washed it.

'I have to find the exact spots to place the electrodes,' she explained. Gently she placed the crown on my head until I could feel the prongs pricking into my scalp. She adjusted each one separately, marking the spot with some kind of pen. Then she removed the instrument and took up the first of the metal electrodes.

'You'll feel a sharp, cold tingling when I attach each one with the acetate. Try not to move.'

It took twenty minutes to get everything in position, and by then I began to realize what women go through to have their hair permed. Eventually all was ready, and she placed a blindfold over one of my eyes.

'Now, this screen which the nurse is lowering in front of you is covered with black and white squares. You'll notice in the centre black square there is a small white dot. Keep your eye on that spot all the time. It will move, sometimes on to a white square when it will disappear, then on to another black square. This will happen at different speeds. At all times focus the eye on the dot. Are you ready?'

Each eye suffered about fifteen minutes of this, until I was getting a splitting headache. The damned spot jiggled around, disappearing then reappearing on another black square, sometimes slowly, then so fast I could hardly follow it. Dr Strombold, who had turned out to be most interesting and pleasant, was finally satisfied.

'Good! Very good! You co-operated beautifully! Now to get these wretched things off. I'm afraid I may have to cut off little bits of your hair.'

With ether and scissors it was eventually accomplished. My scalp felt sore and tingling, and when she gave me a sterilized brush I found most of my hair seemed glued together. The whole operation had taken nearly an hour. One of the nurses helped me back to my wheelchair, and Dr Strombold telephoned through for an orderly.

'How did I do?' I asked. 'Will I pass my exams?'

'I've no idea until we study the printouts. You realize there's nearly a mile of squiggles to examine? Luckily our computer doesn't mind working overtime.'

The nurse wheeled me out to the corridor, said good-bye, and left me to wait for an orderly. I felt like a sack of garbage waiting for the dustmen.

That evening I had my first proper meal. It was only mince and potatoes and cauliflower, but it tasted superb. Some tinned peaches followed, and I lay back afterwards in a pleasantly stuffed euphoria. Alec was bitching, kindly, to Tessa, the coloured nurse.

'For a hospital, the food's quite good. But why bother with that absurd menu when you never receive what you order? There was turkey on the menu this morning. Does this look like turkey? It's steamed haddock. And those soggy, ashamed peas? Do they resemble cauliflower? And that delicious treacle tart I ordered looks suspiciously like tinned pears. All in all, the usual disaster!'

Tessa bravely defended the kitchens deep under the building. 'Do you realize that they have to provide *four thousand* meals a day here? *Hot* meals! Breakfast, lunch and dinner for every patient and member of the staff. I think it's fantastic what they do. You're just a fuss-pot!'

He smiled at her. He really was an attractive fellow, despite his cynical outlook on life. 'I'm only kidding! It's the best bloody hospital in the country, we should be so lucky! But I still wanted turkey.'

I had no trouble going to sleep that night. After my adventurous walk, followed by the strain of watching the little white spot, I felt exhausted. By ten o'clock I was in a dreamless sleep.

I was awakened by the sound of muffled screams and moans. I sat up in alarm, trying to orientate my surroundings. Then I realized the noise was coming from the burn patient at the end of the ward. The screams subsided into snorts and groans and I wondered what despairing thoughts were passing through that tortured brain as he realized he was still alive and horribly burnt.

No longer sleepy, I lay and considered my future. In a week or so I would have to walk out of the hospital, still with my imbalance, and take up a place in society again. I would not produce *Misty Horizon*; it was better to face facts squarely, and the hectic and variable life of a film producer was no longer for me. Physical activity had to be avoided.

Amongst other advice which Mr Garold had given me, I was to lie down for half an hour every afternoon, 'to charge up the batteries', as the concentration needed to keep my balance used up much more energy than the average person would spend.

But, when sitting, I had no balance problem. So why not write? In my younger days I had written short stories and several screenplays. All my life I had been involved with writers. I loved to read, and I knew good writing from bad. At school, my strongest subject had been English literature. Now I had the time and the opportunity to write the Great English Novel.

The idea excited me. I could sell my share in the business, and I still had royalties coming in from previous films. I would move into a smaller apartment, and could live reasonably comfortably for a year or two until my book was published. I knew I was being optimistic, as publishers now were much tougher than in the past, owing to enormous increases in the price of paper. But it was better to be optimistic; no point in discarding the idea before it even gave birth.

The swing doors opened and a gurney was wheeled in silently. I thought at first it carried a huge black man, then I saw in the subdued light it was a man entirely encased in a black plastic sack, leaving only his head free. They wheeled him to one of the two empty beds. A nurse and each of the attendants took two curious instruments in their hands, like huge ping-pong bats, and slid them under the figure. He was then lifted on to the bed, but there was something wrong about the movement. The black sack seemed to roll on to the covers, as if it contained jelly, not the body of a human being. They left him there, without covering the sack or even undoing it, a sinister shining black bag against the whiteness of the bed. It had been Rhoda who had helped the orderlies, and when she passed my bed a few minutes later I called to her softly.

'What happened to him? Is he a burn case?' But I had not heard the air-conditioning being increased, nor smelt that horrible odour of burnt flesh. I hardly expected to get a straight answer, except that in this ward they seemed to encourage mutual exchanges to make other patients aware of their own folly.

Her attractive face made a grimace of distaste. 'Horrible! He fell eight stories on to concrete and is still alive, by a miracle. But they had to scoop up his body into the bag. He must have landed on his feet, his head is hardly damaged.'

I tried not to imagine the details. 'Was it suicide? Or an accident?'

'They found a note, but I don't know the reason.'

'Can they do anything for him?'

'Not a chance. It's only a question of minutes or hours. At least he can't feel anything. Go back to sleep!'

She left me and I listened to the moans of the burn case, rising and falling in a crescendo of agony; wondering if the man in the black bag could actually think, even if he could feel nothing. His brain longing for the welcome release of death. My depression grew and I felt claustrophobic, a sudden urge to run through the swing doors and escape from this nightmare ward.

Suddenly I heard the man next to Alec, who had been slapped by his wife, struggle into a sitting position, his screams cutting through the ward, 'Tell him to stop that bloody noise! Make him stop it! Put the poor bastard out of his agony!' It was the same panicky bedlam which had swept through the ward another night.

Instantly nurses hurried over, making him lie down and soothing him, then giving him an injection. Other nurses circled the ward, reassuring patients who had been awakened, trying to calm the instinctive fear which seemed to spread like a disease when suffering became so raw that it transmitted its own message of agony. Miss Sims came over to me.

'You all right? Try to get back to sleep.'

'He's right though, can't you give something to stop the pain?'

She smiled sadly. 'Believe it or not, it's a good sign, it means his nervous system isn't damaged. But he'll get a sedative, although his burns are too severe to give an injection.'

The case had been brought in the previous night, and even Alec hadn't found out his history. I asked Miss Sims what had happened.

'He poured methylated spirits over himself, then set it on fire. But it burns very quickly and it went out before he could die. His wife heard his screams, so he had immediate attention. But it'll be touch and go.'

It was a tragic thought, but my sympathy for the man waned. I imagined the suffering he had brought to his wife, carrying out such a selfish act, knowing that his own wife, whom he had presumably once married with love and affection, would find his charred body. Oh Lord, thy works are truly mysterious!

Against all my gloomy predictions, I went back to sleep and dreamt of having a happy picnic in glorious sunshine.

By morning Black Sack had died and been removed. It was a sunny day and I felt much stronger. My throat was almost back to normal, and my stomach muscles no longer felt as if they had been mule-kicked. After breakfast I put on my dressing-gown and made my tour of the ward, encouraged by Bossy Boots, who was beginning to think I was a fraud. But I liked her hard-line approach, a no-nonsense attitude which covered a mind as sympathetic as any of the other nurses.

Alec was taken away in a wheelchair and shortly afterwards returned on crutches with his new feet. He had orders to walk with them for an hour a day, gradually to increase this period as he grew used to them. I was happy to note that he seemed more cheerful and I hoped he had given up his idea of killing himself the moment he was released.

I hobbled across to Mr Carstairs. He was lying back against his pillows and looked pale and tired. I asked him how he felt.

'Not so good today. I nearly copped it during the night, the old ticker gets temperamental sometimes. But I'll be fine soon, as soon as these shoulders get better. When are they discharging you?'

'In about a week, I think. I'm feeling much stronger, but

they want to be sure I don't have a relapse; apparently it takes some time to get all the poison out of one's system.' It seemed strange to be discussing one's suicide as if it was a mild case of 'flu, but I no longer felt any embarrassment. That would come later when I faced people in the outside world who might shy away from me in pity.

'You made any plans for the future?'

'Not really. Dr Marshall says I must take it very easy for at least a month, get lots of fresh air, get myself properly adjusted. But maybe I'll take up writing, I used to be quite good at it.'

'I'll watch for your bestsellers! Perhaps you'll become another Graham Greene.'

'My favourite author! No, I could never aspire to his standards, I'd just settle to be a poor man's Harold Robbins, with a couple of big yachts on the Riviera.'

'I would have liked to write. But I suppose everyone has that secret ambition. I was a frogman during the war, had some hair-raising experiences; perhaps one day I'll try to write it all down. You'll be too famous by then to "ghost" it for me!'

I grinned. 'That'll be the day! You're very kind, I feel encouraged already. If I ever get published I'll send you an autographed copy.' Casually I watched the green blip on his heart machine; it looked very unhealthy.

I circled the ward, saying hullo to the conscious patients. I avoided the vegetable patient; there was something horrible about his open eyes, staring endlessly at the ceiling. Physically, apparently, there was little wrong with him, but his brain was dead. What would become of him? Would they allow him to live for years, or would they mercifully stop his heart? I now felt very strongly in favour of euthanasia, although I knew the old arguments would continue to rage until some adventurous soul managed to change the law. I wished some of the anti-mercy-killing people could spend a few days in The Graveyard and realize how intensely cruel it was to keep alive some of these broken and tortured patients.

Dr Marshall arrived for her rounds.

'You're to see Mr Brackett today. I've made an appointment for two o'clock.'

'Who's Mr Brackett? Do I owe him money?'

She was writing in my chart, laughing. 'Mr Brackett is our distinguished Chief Neurologist. He has Dr Payne's report on you, also the results of your neurology tests.'

'Ah, the chief beak, the headmaster! I hope he has more charm than Mr Garold!'

'Garold's all right, just a bit dry. He's very brilliant, one of the top E.N.T. men in the country. Anyway, Mr Brackett is a poppet, you'll like him.'

Later in the morning I noticed Mr Perry having an argument with Gladys. Finally, exasperated, she came over to me.

'I'm sorry, but will you do me a favour? Mr Perry has been allowed up and he managed to walk round the ward yesterday. Now he refuses to use a bedpan and wants to go to the toilet. But he won't let me help him, he wants *you* to help him!'

I couldn't help laughing, but I saw Mr Perry anxiously watching and tried to keep my face serious. 'Of course I will, but it's the blind leading the blind. Stick close in case we both fall over!'

I stood up and reached for my stick. Mr Perry gleefully climbed out of bed and stood swaying until I gave him my arm. Like a couple of drunks we shuffled down to the toilets, Gladys following anxiously behind. At the door to a loo the old man thanked me and allowed the nurse to take over. I returned to find the Floor Matron waiting for me, with Jerri beside her.

'You can have a shower today,' she boomed. 'Get all that sticky mess out of your hair, you'll feel better for it. But Nurse must be with you all the time.'

'*All* the time?' I said in mock dismay, although the thought of a shower was like entering Paradise. 'I might get an erection!'

Jerri giggled; Matron glared.

'We're not interested in your lascivious sex life,' she said cuttingly. 'One complaint from her and I'll cut the miserable thing off!'

It's impossible to describe the sheer bliss of that shower. Although I had a sponge bath every day I always felt itchy and uncomfortable by the evening, and my head had felt clogged up since the neurology tests. I stood under the warm water and soaped myself all over, feeling my scalp return to normal and my body tingling with freshness. Even Jerri standing in front of me making rude wisecracks didn't bother me; with Rhoda I just might have been more embarrassed. Afterwards, she changed my wet dressings and put on new ones.

A few minutes before two, Fred collected me with his wheelchair. I was feeling so much better, both morally and physically, that I almost jumped into it. Fred remarked on my recovery as we sped down the corridors.

'Yer gittin' well, aren't yer! That's the trouble 'ere, mate, yer no sooner gits to know someone than they're either leavin' or they're dead!'

Mr Brackett had an imposing office, but I liked him immediately. He was in his forties, smoking a pipe, and he came from behind his desk and indicated we sit in two armchairs in front of the unlit fire. Sun-shafts, opening like a Japanese fan, streamed in the large window, picking up little motes of dust and illuminating the Adam fireplace.

'Sit down, old fellow, you're looking remarkably healthy!'

'I'm feeling much better, especially after having a shower. I loathe feeling dirty.'

He puffed smoke in my direction. It smelt of a delicious Balkan Sobranie. He consulted a file he had placed on his knee.

'Well, what have we here. I suppose you realize you're a very unusual case?'

'I feel ashamed to have caused all this trouble. I never dreamed I might still live.'

'You've no right to be alive. You took three times the fatal dose, and you weren't even discovered quickly. I think you could qualify for the *Guinness Book of Records,* or at least an article in the *Medical Journal*!'

'How do you think it happened? There's a poor bastard in my ward who did the same thing, and he's apparently a vegetable.'

'Yes, unfortunately, that's always the danger. In your case it was several lucky reasons. First of all, you have an abnormally strong heart, which despite everything kept on beating, apart from your relapse last Friday. Secondly, you're in pretty good health, which helps. Thirdly, the large dinner you ate was undigested, therefore it helped to "mop up" the poison and stop it spreading too quickly. Fourthly, you went to bed after a bath, so there was almost no dirt or germs to help the breakdown of tissue. Even allowing for all that, you had the luck of the devil. Your brain cells are undamaged, which is almost a miracle in itself.'

I thought of Pete and his miracles. When I was discharged, I'd try to see a lot more of him.

'So,' continued Mr Brackett, 'your tests yesterday were completely positive. Normal eye reaction, maybe a little above normal, so your balance situation is confined entirely to one ear, the left one. The stapedectomy obviously was the cause of it; somewhere along the line the perilymph leaked. The operation itself was a success, the teflon piston which was fitted has restored your hearing. In other words, the loss of balance only occurs in one ear, so it's not a *complete* loss of balance.'

'But there's nothing that can be done about it?'

'No, I'm afraid not. But I've studied both Mr Garold's report and Dr Payne's, and it would appear your main reason to try suicide was a fear it would degenerate to an extent where you would not be able to walk. Is that correct?'

'Yes. The last specialist I went to see said I must be prepared for the possibility of ending up in a wheelchair.'

Mr Brackett looked angry for a moment. 'Stuff and nonsense! I won't ask who it was, but it was not a wise remark. I can tell you positively that it is highly unlikely it will become worse. On the contrary, it could ease a little as the years pass, and certainly you'll become more used to it.'

'You mean I'll learn to live with it?' I said with a straight face. He grinned suddenly like a mischievous schoolboy.

'I never use that expression, it's much too easy and incredibly pompous. But, yes, in this case you will, just like having false teeth or losing a finger or even having a heart attack. After a few months, or a year or two, you'll never even think about it. The human body has a superb way of adapting to new circumstances.'

I felt enormously relieved. It was possible he was giving me a snow job, but I didn't think so. My suicide attempt now seemed ridiculous and shameful.

'What I suggest is this,' he went on. 'I gather that your financial circumstances are not strained, so go away, into the country if possible, and first of all get your strength back and let those scars heal. Think a bit about your future life; you could have another forty years ahead of you. Don't try to build Rome in a day, or attempt to prove anything. You're never going to become a steeplejack, nor are you going to win the hundred yard sprint. Just concentrate on what you *can* do, what you *want* to do. And every time you get depressed because you can't play tennis or squash, just think of some of those patients upstairs and what faces them in their life ahead.'

He closed the file with a snap and stood up.

'I don't have to lecture you! You're cured, fit, and ready to go. We'll keep you here for another week, just to monitor your recovery in case any infection sets in, which is highly unlikely now; then you're on your own!'

I returned to the ward a much happier man. I realized that ever since I had regained consciousness in the Intensive Care Unit my confidence and temperament had been extremely low. I had felt scared of everyone, like a shy new schoolboy terrified of incurring the disapproval of authority; feeling guilty about still being alive.

Now I was almost ready to face the world again. Of course, it would be difficult and embarrassing at times. The average person is subconsciously afraid of a failed suicide, afraid that a wrong word or a misunderstood slight may cause him to try again. It would be up to me to overcome this feeling amongst my friends. What friends, I wondered? I had behaved so boorishly over the past year that I had few of them left. Perhaps I should go abroad to start my book, cultivate a new life and new acquaintances, make myself the life and soul of the party. I decided to take Mr Brackett's advice and not try to rush into heavy decisions.

Still, it was good to be alive.

Epilogue

That's almost the end of my story.

Each day I became stronger. My appetite was excellent and I gobbled up whatever was put in front of me, which, as Alec rightly had said, was seldom what one ordered from the menu brought round every morning. I was twenty pounds lighter than the night I had taken the pills, and I meant to stay that way. I read a great deal, and several times a day I would wander around the ward, doing what I could to help, passing out books or newspapers, talking to the conscious patients, emptying ashtrays, and generally getting in the way. My pride and joy was the responsibility of making tea and coffee and being the official tea-boy.

I still had my balance problem, but now I was determined to overcome it and eventually ignore it. I learnt not to turn my head sharply or look upwards, which always caused the room to revolve for a second. I tried never to bend down without support from my stick. There was no way I would give in to this ridiculous imbalance.

Alec was growing used to his new feet and could now move carefully around without his crutches. He was to be discharged shortly after me, and I took his address and promised to telephone him when I had made contact with some useful television or radio producers. He seemed in good spirits and sometimes helped me with the tea trolley. We developed a mock-quarrel double act about the quality of the tea and coffee which amused some of the patients and had the nurses in hysterics.

Mr Carstairs improved and the cast round his neck and shoulders was removed. As far as I knew he had not had another emergency with his heart. We had many long talks and he told me some enthralling tales of his work. I hoped he would eventually write his memoirs.

Mr Perry improved beyond recognition. He was now a kindly old man, eager to get back to his daughter and son-in-law and start growing his beloved roses. He was allowed to get dressed and each day a nurse walked him round the hospital grounds. He still had an embarrassing adoration towards me, and kept promising me he would write often and keep in touch. I promised to do the same.

The little Scotsman had left, under protest, but apparently had arrived safely in Glasgow. I think Dr Payne had finally scared him not to attempt another phoney suicide, as his last attempt had just missed an artery in his wrist. No doubt he would eventually end up in a Glasgow hospital. He had appeared quite incorrigible but one could only feel a liking for him.

Rhoda had shattered my hopes by announcing her engagement. I would have to find romance elsewhere. Meanwhile, during the long strained hours of the night the ceaseless flow of human wreckage, smashed and bloodied, came and went, a despairing reflection on human weakness. I still felt part of the ward, but as I grew stronger I became impatient to depart.

On the day before I was due to leave I had an examination by Drs Marshall and Payne. They banged and thumped and pricked me, and carefully examined my sores, which were healing slowly. They appeared satisfied.

'Well, tomorrow's the big day,' said my lovely Dr Marshall. 'We'll miss you, there have been no complaints about the tea or coffee since you took over.'

'Thanks a bunch,' I said sourly. 'Maybe the hospital will give me regular employment!'

'Seriously,' she said, 'you've done a good job on yourself. Just keep it up. I'll want to see you in about three weeks' time, just to make sure everything is healing well. Will you ring me to make an appointment?'

'Only on one condition! If I come all the way up from the country just to satisfy your ego, will you have lunch with me?'

'All things being equal, I will! I've never seen you with clothes on!'

She looked very lovely that morning, but I knew from my source-of-all-information, Alec, that she was married to another doctor. If he worked as hard as she did, I wondered if they ever met.

Josh had been to see me, faithful Josh who hated hospitals, and I had asked him to bring in two large boxes of chocolates and a big plant. That night I gave a box to the night staff, and the plant, a quite magnificent fuchsia, stood on top of the control board. In the morning, as each nurse went off duty, she came across to wish me luck. In some ways I felt very sad, realizing that once I left the hospital they would fade into a memory of the past; they had their lives to lead, just as I would have mine.

I had agreed to stay with some friends who lived in the country. I had not seen them for two years, but Josh had made the arrangements discreetly, saying I was recovering from a nervous breakdown. They were very kindly driving to town to pick me up at midday.

At nine o'clock I had my shower, and Gladys, who had just come on duty, changed my dressings for the last time. She presented me with a large packet of gauze, some ointment, and surgical tape.

'Don't forget,' she admonished me, 'after you take a bath, you change the dressings. For at least ten days. Don't risk getting any dirt on them.' Then she took scissors and cut off the name tag round my wrist. Now I really *was* free!

She brought my suitcase and clothes, which Josh had lugged over from my apartment the day before, and I slowly dressed. It was strange to feel the texture of a shirt again, and the familiar feeling of knotting a tie. My shoes hurt, and my suit felt stiff and uncomfortable. I packed my books and notes and other belongings, and made my last tour of the ward to say good-bye.

I presented the other box of chocolates to the Floor Matron, and sat down to wait for another half hour until midday, feeling slightly foolish and embarrassed. Some of the patients would only leave the ward on gurneys with sheets over their faces, others would leave in a wheelchair, scarred for life. I was the fortunate one.

At ten to twelve the nurse on the control board called out to me: 'Your friends are downstairs; a nurse will take you down to the entrance in a wheelchair. Your suitcase will be waiting for you.'

I waved to the ward in general, then self-consciously sat in the wheelchair brought in by a smiling girl. As we reached the swing doors there was a sinister *thunk* and the red light went on over Mr Carstairs's bed. Unbelievingly I looked at the screen beside him and saw only a straight flat line. The green blip was still. Mr Carstairs would never write his memoirs.

I walked through the doors into the world again.